THE
COMPLETE
CAT
BOOK

THE
COMPLETE
CAT
BOOK

~

Paddy Cutts

SMITHMARK

This edition published in 1992 by
SMITHMARK Publishers Inc.
16 East 32nd Street
New York, NY 10016

© 1992 Anness Publishing Limited
Boundary Row Studios
1 Boundary Row
London SE1 8HP

Reprinted in 1994

ISBN 0-8317-8194-7

Editorial Director: Joanna Lorenz
Project Editor: Judith Simons
Editor: Lesley Ellis
Art Director: Peter Bridgewater
Designer: Annie Moss
Illustrator: Vana Haggerty

SMITHMARK books are available for bulk purchase
for sales promotion and premium use. For details
write or call the manager of special sales,
SMITHMARK Publishers Inc., 16 East 32nd Street
New York, NY 10016; (212) 532-6600.

Printed and bound in Hong Kong

CONTENTS

CAT CHARACTERISTICS

The cat is probably the single most popular pet in the world today. Why this is, is open to speculation. Cats are not obedient like dogs; we cannot train them to perform tricks or bring slippers. They no longer work for us as mousers. They are independent, and always give the impression that they do not need us for survival. They possess a mystique — we may think that we understand our cat, but do we really? Cats seem to have an expression that says 'You may think that you know me, but I really know better'. Just what it is that makes a cat a cat is difficult to describe. Ask anybody who has had the privilege of sharing their home with a fickle feline and they will each give you a different answer.

THE HISTORY OF THE DOMESTIC CAT

Throughout history, the cat has been subject to several ups and downs in the popularity stakes.

Some of the earliest evidence of the domestic cat are to be found in Ancient Egypt, where it was worshipped as a god, and where the penalty for killing a cat was death. Cats were buried with the ceremony befitting a pharoah and it was common to mummify not just kings, but cats too. It is from these mummified felines that we have been able to learn much about the early domesticated cat. The British Museum in London holds

The cat was a highly revered creature in Ancient Egypt as it was seen as the earthly embodiment of the cat goddess, Bast. Mummified remains reveal that this early domesticated cat sported a brownish ticked or tabby coat, as can be seen in these Egyptian wall paintings: a small cat crouches under a stool watching a chess-playing couple (**ABOVE**); *a feline* (**LEFT**) *accompanies a family on a hunting expedition, flushing out fowl from the Nile marsh (from Thebes, c 1400 BC).*

booty from the raids carried out on pyramids at the turn of the century, including many mummified cats. When the bandages were removed, the cats were all found to be quite similar: small short-haired cats with brownish 'ticked' coats, rather similar to the breed we now call the Abyssinian.

Once worshipped as gods, the tide changed for the cat during the Middle Ages, when it was considered to be a witch's 'familiar'. Both witch and cat suffered the same fate, and were burned to death. The black cat has always been associated with witchcraft and from this, certain superstitions have arisen. A black cat crossing your path is supposed to be a bad omen, although some people in contrast consider a black cat to be a lucky mascot – wires have certainly got crossed somewhere along the line.

In Burma and Thailand, cats have always been held in high esteem. Breeds that we know today as Burmese, Siamese and Korat owe their ancestry to these far-off parts of the world. The Siamese was known as the 'Royal' Cat of Siam, and only royalty were allowed to own such a cat. It was considered an honour to be given one, and they were usually only bestowed on visiting dignitaries from

ABOVE
Cat with Fish; Indian Kalighat.

RIGHT
Kitten and Ball of Wool, by Murata Kokodu, 1866. This delightful Japanese painting shows a cat with the markings and short tail associated with the Japanese Bobtail breed.

LEFT
Yoshifuji, Witch Cat of Okabe on Tokkaido Road. This mischievous pair of cats show the classic mi-ke coloration of white, red and black.

ABOVE

The Manx is one of the best known of the tail-less varieties of pedigree cat. Indigenous to the Isle of Man, off the west coast of England, and popular worldwide, this breed has evolved through a limited gene pool restricted to the cat population of this remote island.

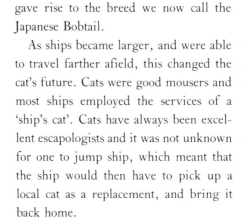

other countries who had won favour with the king. Perhaps because of the limited gene pool available in such remote regions these cats often had deformed tails.

Similar inbreeding was seen in Japan; isolated on an island, the indigenous cat population did not have the chance to mate with unrelated cats and so any fault in the genetic make-up would have been doubled up with each generation. This gave rise to the breed we now call the Japanese Bobtail.

As ships became larger, and were able to travel farther afield, this changed the cat's future. Cats were good mousers and most ships employed the services of a 'ship's cat'. Cats have always been excellent escapologists and it was not unknown for one to jump ship, which meant that the ship would then have to pick up a local cat as a replacement, and bring it back home.

Off the west coast of England, near the port of Liverpool, is the Isle of Man, a small island which is home to a tail-less variety of cat known as the Manx. It is thought that these tail-less cats first came to the island on ships from the Far East; stormy weather sometimes caused the ships to stop at the Isle of Man as they were unable to get into Liverpool, and it is quite likely that the occasional cat jumped ship here. As the island had little trading or contact with the mainland, these cats were free to breed only with each other and so the tail-less factor was increased. Even today, most cats on Man are tail-less, although they do produce the occasional tailed kitten.

THE EVOLUTION OF THE DOMESTIC CAT

All cats are descended from their larger, wild relations and some of this heritage can still be seen in the modern domestic cat, whether pedigree or moggie.

Evolution has given the cat a camouflaged coat so that it is hidden from predators. In the wild, the cat's natural instinct is to sleep by day and hunt under cover of darkness. A visit to the zoo will confirm just how successful this camouflage has been: lions, living in dry regions with sparse vegetation, have adopted a sandy colour to their coat; snow leopards are pale to blend with their snowy environment; jungle cats are usually spotted or striped, echoing the dappled light that illuminates the forest floor. Just as clever is the coat of the domestic tortoiseshell cat – for a female rearing her young, a camouflaged coat is important, and a tortie pattern makes her almost indistinguishable from the background in a variety of locations. The tortoiseshell gene is sex-linked for this purpose, occurring usually only in female cats.

As cats tend to sleep by day, they have evolved another mechanism as well as coat colour to defend themselves, and this can still be seen in the domestic cat today. Cats have very little fur between the top of their eyes and their ears. Look at a cat

Continued page 13

RIGHT
In the wild, camouflage is all-important to conceal animals from predators. Domestic cats, as well as their larger wild cousins, display coat patterns and colours designed to blend into their natural habitats. This tortoiseshell is almost imperceptible against the surroundings of the garden.

LEFT
This sleeping Burmese cat gives the appearance of being awake, even though the eyes are tightly shut. The thin patches of fur immediately above the eyes will confuse a predator into thinking that the cat is alert and on guard.

WILD CATS

LEFT
The kittens of the Indian Desert Cat show distinct spots, but these fade in maturity.

A sk any cat owner why they choose to share their life with a domestic feline, and the answer is often that they admire the cat's independent streak. This trait can be directly related back to its wild cat ancestry, that self-sufficient, superbly designed creature that has adapted itself to life in all corners of the world; hot or cold climates, snow or sun, rain forest or desert, mountain or flat land, there has always been a feline of some description that has adapted to the environment.

BELOW
The Scottish Wild Cat has developed a thick, waterproof coat as a protection against harsh weather, and a fearsome expression to ward off predators.

LEFT
The name Jungle Cat is a slight misnomer as the cat originally evolved in the sandy area of Egypt, and has a pale, ticked coat colour suitable for camouflage in desert regions.

RIGHT
Leopard Cat is the common term for the La-Lang cat. The natural habitat for the species is dark forests and regions of long grass, hence the need for large eyes, and the spotted coat reflects the natural dappled light pattern that would fall on the forest floor.

ABOVE
The Siamese originates from the warm tropics and its typical smooth, silky and light-coloured coat allows the cat to cool quickly in extreme heat.

when it is asleep, and the bald area gives the impression of open eyes, so that any predator will think the cat is wide awake, on guard and ready to attack. It is a simple, but effective, form of protection.

The length and type of fur depends on which part of the world the cat originates from. The Scottish Wild Cat has a thick, dense coat which keeps it warm and dry in the bleakest of Scottish winters. Persians and Angoras, native to the upland regions of Iran and Turkey, developed long coats for the same reason; mountainous regions get cold at night and in the winter, and the extra long coat has an insulating effect. Pale-coated Siamese have a fine silky texture to their coat allowing them to cool rapidly when the weather is hot. Russian Blues, originally thought to have come from Archangel

(Archangel'sk), have a curious 'double' coat, to keep them warm in Baltic climes.

Cats have been imported and exported for many decades and so do not always end up living in a climate suited to their type of fur. It is for this reason that owners of longhaired cats in tropical regions sometimes clip the long fur down during the hotter parts of the year, and that varieties from the Far East living in cooler areas benefit from additional heating during the cold seasons.

◦ CAT BEHAVIOUR ◦

Much of the behaviour that the modern domestic cat displays directly relates to its wild origins. This is not always socially acceptable, but cats are

ABOVE
Burmese are an adaptable and sturdy breed. The very first Burmese did indeed come from Burma, but today they are quite acclimatized to the more severe winters of northern regions.

BELOW
The ever-popular Persian was first seen in the northern upland regions of Iran. With freezing temperatures at night and during winter, cats from this area needed thick coats to help keep them warm.

very territorial and much of what they do reflects their need to stake out territory, especially if they are not neutered.

In the wild, this territorial behaviour is important. In times of famine or drought, there is little food to go around and the male stakes out territory to ensure that intruders do not come and raid his particular area of available prey. If he has a female with kittens this is even more important, if the kittens are to survive. It is not unknown for a male cat to attack the young of another cat. This is still true today – a maurauding tom cat can easily kill a defenceless young kitten in your own back garden.

Cats like to mark out their territory with chemical messages; these tell any other cat that strays into the area to 'keep off'. The most common way of marking

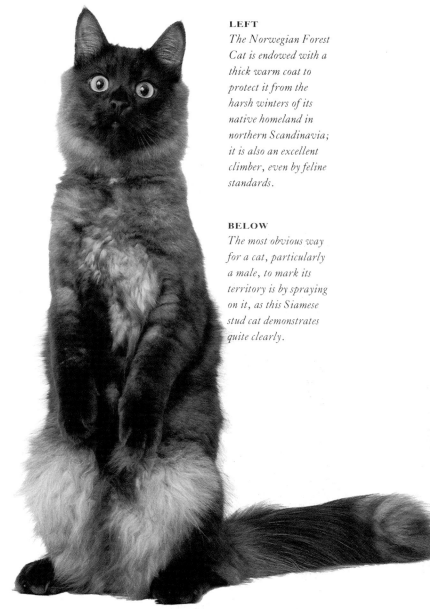

The Norwegian Forest Cat is endowed with a thick warm coat to protect it from the harsh winters of its native homeland in northern Scandinavia; it is also an excellent climber, even by feline standards.

BELOW

The most obvious way for a cat, particularly a male, to mark its territory is by spraying on it, as this Siamese stud cat demonstrates quite clearly.

ABOVE

Cats like to mark their 'property' with scent, which can be done in many ways. Glands behind the cat's ears will exude a smell particular to the cat, but imperceptible to humans. In this case the resident human has been considered worthy of being 'marked' in this way!

is by spraying concentrated urine around the boundaries of the territory. To humans, this is one of the most unpleasant smells we know and is usually associated with the entire male; another good reason for neutering. However, entire females – especially when on call – and even some neutered cats, will also spray. Cats that have been confined indoors during the cold winter months will probably spray all four corners of the garden when they are allowed out in the spring. Frost will have destroyed any trace of the previous territorial markings, and so the cat has to 'beat the bounds' of his territory before another cat lays claim to his patch.

As long as this activity is confined to the outdoors, it does not affect us too much; it is only when a cat starts to spray inside the house that it becomes socially unacceptable for us, although it makes perfect sense to the cat. It is not common for the well-adjusted, socially integrated and neutered cat to spray indoors, but it can happen.

The most common reason for a cat to spray indoors is when another feline is introduced to the household. The resident

cat sees it as a threat and will mark out 'his' home with his own personal scent. This can even happen if a piece of secondhand furniture is brought into the house that smells of another cat; the resident cat's instinct is to spray it just to be sure that it is adequately marked as part of his own home.

Cats also mark territory and leave chemical messages in other, more acceptable, ways. The cat has glands that secrete scent in several parts of their bodies, particularly around the back of the head. When a cat comes and rubs its head against your leg, it is actually marking you; the message it leaves is for other cats, and translates roughly as 'This is my human; keep away'. For the same reason, cats rub against domestic objects such as

LEFT
Even the domesticated entire male will feel the need to patrol its territory, often spraying to warn other male cats to keep away from its 'patch'.

ABOVE
Cats have scent glands in their paws, too, and when stropping a tree to sharpen their claws, they will be leaving messages for other cats at the same time.

furniture; they are marking their possessions, but in an inoffensive way.

The same behaviour can be seen outside in the garden, but takes more the part of a conversation between neighbouring cats as they leave messages for each other in a kind of 'dead letter box'. Rubbing against walls, trees and fences the cat can let the local feline population know what is going on: 'Susie' is on call at the moment or 'Sam' has just been neutered . . . . Even when a cat strops a tree to sharpen its claws, it leaves behind a message that comes from glands situated between the paw pads.

Male cats prowl, especially at night, calling for a female; the female on call will make just as much, if not more, noise. It is during these nocturnal forays

BELOW

This cat is picking up a 'message' which another cat has left on the wall.

An intimidated or frightened cat will try to make itself look larger in front of the aggressor by fluffing up its coat, particularly the tail.

A cat on the attack will adopt an aggressive stance: whiskers bristle, muscles are taut, and the cat is lying low ready to pounce.

A cat that rolls over and exposes the most vulnerable part of its anatomy, the stomach area, is submitting to the aggressor.

Crouching low, the cat surveys its prey.

Stealthily, the cat edges nearer.

Suddenly rising up, the cat pounces, ready for the kill.

Mission accomplished, and the cat has caught the mouse.

that a cat is most likely to get into a fight with another, as both are out looking for the same thing – a female to mate. In order to keep peace with the neighbours, and avoid expensive visits to the vet, most owners decide to neuter any cat that is a family pet and keep it in at night.

THE CAT IN THE HOME TODAY

Although we consider the cat to be a domesticated pet, this is not really so. No matter what restrictions we impose on our pets, they are still essentially cats and will always display a certain amount of wild cat behaviour. We can neuter them, keep them safely confined indoors and well fed, but they will still have the roaming instinct, and will want to hunt and catch prey even if they have just finished a meal. This is something that we cannot change; ask any cat lover and, if they answer honestly, they would not want to change it. Part of the charm of living with a cat is that it is probably the nearest most of us will ever get to sharing our home with a small, wild creature. If you want an obedient, well-behaved, dependable and loyal follower, choose a dog. If you want a lifelong friend that chooses you, will offer companionship and sense your every mood instinctively, while still retaining an independent streak, then a cat is for you.

RIGHT
Cats are very much creatures of habit and believe in a serious afternoon 'siesta' during the hotter months; this sensible cat has chosen a shady area for a snooze.

LEFT
The feline species is fastidious and a large part of a cat's day is spent grooming in order to keep its coat in pristine condition.

CAT SENSES

As natural nocturnal hunters, cats have evolved their sense organs to a highly tuned degree. Not only do these senses serve to aid hunting, but also to keep the cat safe from predators. Even though most cats today live in a safe, domestic environment, they still display many characteristics that they developed when the need to hunt for food and day-to-day survival was an important part of their lifestyle.

BELOW
In bright light a cat's pupils will contract to the narrowest of slits. Equally, in dim light they can dilate to a much greater degree than in humans, allowing cats to see better in low light levels.

• SIGHT •

It is not true that cats can see in the dark; with no illumination they can see no better than we can. However, it is true to say that they can see better than humans in low light levels. The feline eye is constructed differently to a human one: the eyeball is rounder with the lens and cornea closer to the retina, allowing the cat to focus more closely than we can; the pupil is capable of dilating to a much greater degree, so admitting more light to the retina and enabling the cat to see better in dim light; and the location of the eyes, which are set wider apart than ours, allows the cat a wider field of vision.

• HEARING •

Although the size of the feline ear varies considerably, they are always set on the head, rather than on either side of the face like humans and monkeys. The external ear organ, the pinna, is movable allowing for directional location of sound. The inner ear has larger echo chambers, so the cat can detect sounds imperceptible to humans, such as those emitted on very high and low frequencies.

BELOW
Set on the head rather than either side of the face, the cat's ears are movable allowing for directional location of sound. The pinna, or external ear, varies in size and is quite large in the Siamese breed.

How, and why, cats purr is debatable; in truth, nobody has scientifically discovered the whys and wherefores of this distinctly feline phenomenon. However here are some ideas.

It is thought that the cat's purr is the result of an electrical impulse generated by the brain, transferred to and carried by the central nervous system, causing certain muscles, particularly those located near the voice box, to contract and thus resonate. The end product, the purr, is felt as a vibration throughout the body but is particularly audible from nose and mouth.

As to why cats purr, this is a different story and these are some theories:

● *It helps increase the efficiency of the circulatory system, and so keeps the cat healthy.*

● *A soft purr is a demand, and a loud one a thank-you message to indicate that the cat has received what it wanted, usually food!*

● *It is a reassuring signal from mother to kitten.*

● *It is a signal from kitten to mother that all is well.*

● *A dominant cat will purr at a subservient one to show that it is not on the attack.*

● *Cats purr when frightened or about to be attacked to say that they are small, defenceless creatures that pose no threat.*

● *Sick, ill or injured cats purr to comfort themselves and to tell others that they are poorly.*

● *The purr is an indication of a pleasured, happy, content cat; this is probably the most popular reason for the purr, an answer most cats would agree with. Purr, and your owner will most likely give you what you want, even if it is the last prawn on the dinner table – cats are not stupid.*

● SCENT ●

The feline nose has olefactory receptors, extremely specialized organs, that can detect minute or extremely low concentrations of substances in the air. They transmit the information they receive to the olefactory lobes in the brain where the scents are recognized and acted upon. The olefactory lobes in animals are physically bigger, pro rata, than in man where they are almost vestigial.

● FLEHMING ●

Flehming is a reaction seen in many mammals. It causes the lips to curl back thus allowing more chemical aromas to register in the Jacobson's Organ. This is situated in the roof of the mouth and, in wild cats, affords the cat an additional method of knowing the 'lie of the land' and what other, possibly predatory, animals lurk nearby. In the domestic cat, this is not of such vital importance as with its wild brethren, and so the flehming reaction is not so obvious.

ABOVE
A cat on the prowl uses its refined sense of smell to locate scents left by other cats.

LEFT
'Flehming' is a reaction whereby the cat curls its lips back to absorb certain chemical aromas and scents, left by other cats, more efficiently into the Jacobson's organ. This is situated in the roof of the mouth and is lined with olefactory cells connected to the part of the brain concerned with sexual behaviour and appetite.

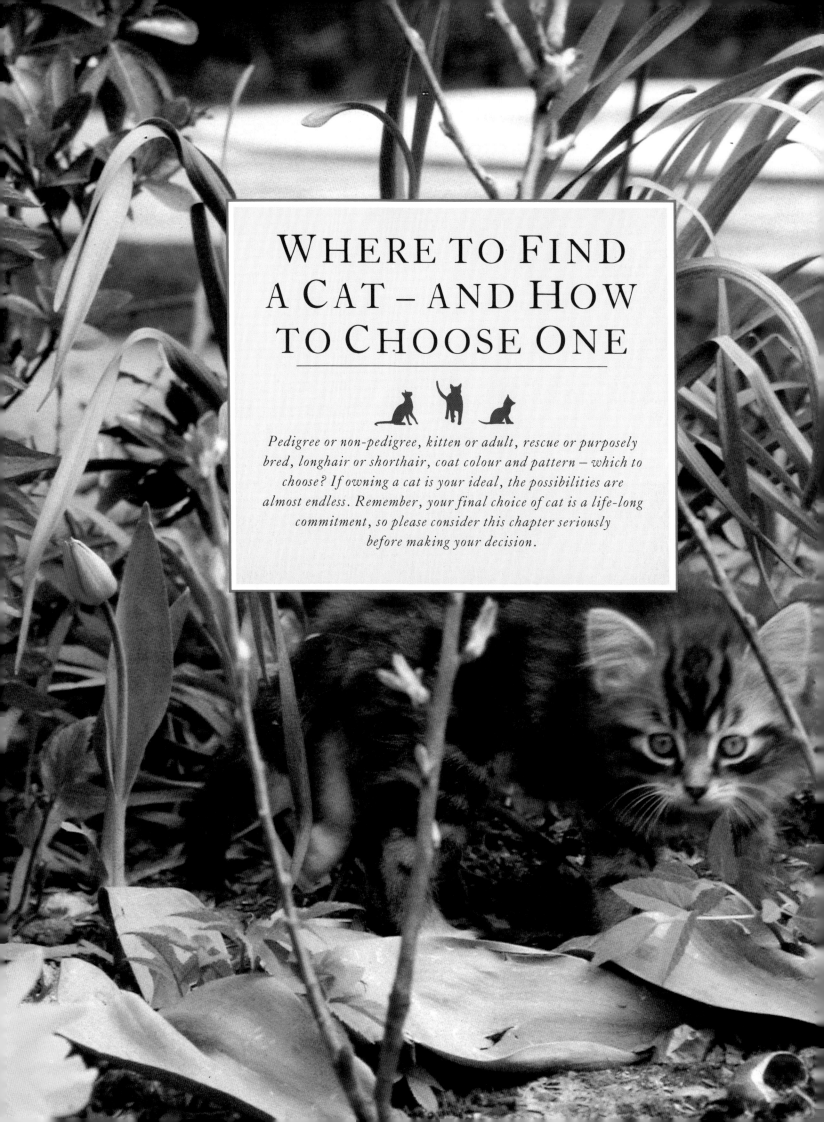

WHERE TO FIND A CAT – AND HOW TO CHOOSE ONE

Pedigree or non-pedigree, kitten or adult, rescue or purposely bred, longhair or shorthair, coat colour and pattern – which to choose? If owning a cat is your ideal, the possibilities are almost endless. Remember, your final choice of cat is a life-long commitment, so please consider this chapter seriously before making your decision.

ABOVE
Cute, fluffy kittens mature into full-grown adults all too soon and responsible ownership entails both time and effort. Longhaired Persians are attractive cats and make affectionate family pets, but their long coats require daily grooming.

RIGHT
Once away from its mother, even a shorthaired kitten will benefit from a regular grooming session with its new owner.

Before making a firm decision to buy a cat do bear the following in mind. Remember that a cat is a life-long undertaking; it can live for twenty years or more – as long as most children stay in the parental 'nest'. Most people think seriously before starting a family, and the adoption of a cat should also be considered very carefully. That cute, fluffy kitten bought on the spur of the moment will soon grow into an adult. It will need annual inoculations, spaying or neutering at about six to nine months, and possible veterinary treatment for illness. There is no free medical care for cats; some charities will help out in deserving cases, but basically think of your veterinary surgeon as a fairly expensive private doctor.

You will also probably want to take holidays and good boarding catteries are not cheap. Two English friends of mine with eight cats used to visit their son in Australia each year; they saved enough for the price of three return tickets, as the cost of boarding their cats amounted to a return trip to Sydney from London. If cost alone has not put you off the thought of sharing your life with a cat, read on.

All cats require grooming, but especially if they are longhaired. This takes time. Shorthaired cats benefit from a regular brush and comb, but longhairs need grooming for at least fifteen minutes a day to prevent the fur becoming tangled. This applies to non-pedigree cats as well as their more aristocratic relations.

It is very tempting to give in to children, especially at Christmas, and agree to give a kitten as a present. These kittens too often become the abandoned felines taken in to rescue centres in the New Year. The decision to share your home with a cat should be made only after a full family discussion. Consider who will clean the litter tray, feed the cat, be responsible for it, and pay the bills.

The Canine Defence League, in the UK, provides bumper stickers which read 'A puppy is for life, not just for

Cats can have a most therapeutic effect on their owners, especially if they are elderly. The cat's soothing purr, encouraged by gentle stroking, is known to lower the blood pressure and thus prevent heart problems. Constantly demanding, the cat will help to keep an older person active and make him or her get up out of the chair and prepare a suitable feline repast!

BELOW

If it is not important for your family to have a kitten, think seriously about taking in an adult rescue. It may take a little longer to settle in, as it will be more set in its ways, but will reward you with its friendship and companionship.

ABOVE

Cats and children can make ideal companions. However, before purchasing a cat or kitten, it is important that the whole family is aware of the responsibilities and duties involved.

Christmas'. This should also be the motto for kittens: *never* give a kitten as a present to somebody without consulting them first; they may well like other people's cats, but might not want the responsibility of a pet of their own.

If by now you are not completely put off by the moral responsibility and indeed the expense of owning a pet, you must now decide what sort of cat you want: pedigree or non-pedigree, adult or kitten. There are many responsible ways to acquire a cat so, *if* you have firmly decided that you want one, consider the possibilities.

First, a word of warning. The most obvious place to buy a new pet would seem to be the local pet store. But, although pet stores are ideal for providing all the accoutrements for your new feline friend, they are hardly the right environment for a creature to grow up in. Pet shop kittens are likely to have been taken away from their mother too early and may be offered for sale when they are not even old enough to be wormed or to have the necessary inoculations. This makes them particularly vulnerable to

any infectious illness, and could result in expensive vet's bills, and even death. Pedigree kittens in pet shops are usually the result of greedy breeders over-breeding their stock. No reputable cat breeder would even consider selling to a pet shop.

NON-PEDIGREE KITTENS

Moggies come in such a multitude of shapes, sizes, patterns, colours and varying length of fur that you can be spoiled for choice. Many can look extremely glamorous and, as their parentage is often unknown, may have a pedigree cat in their background.

The most obvious way to find a kitten is by word of mouth. In the summer months there are usually kittens looking for new homes but, fortunately, not as

♦ ONE KITTEN OR TWO? ♦

Consider your living and working arrangements. Is the home unoccupied for most of the day, or is there usually somebody at home? No young creature likes to be left on its own all day so, if you are out at work for any length of time, think about getting two kittens which will be company for each other. If you have to board them when you take a holiday, they will give each

other companionship. A bored kitten may attack the carpets and curtains while you are at work, not to mention the houseplants and ornaments; two kittens will play with each other and spare you the expense of refurnishing your house and replacing valuables. You would hardly expect a human toddler to behave perfectly, so why expect more of a kitten?

For owners who are out at work all day but still wish for a cat, the sensible and responsible choice is to take two kittens, preferably from the same litter (ABOVE).

They will feel less nervous when introduced to their new home and will be companions for each other as they grow up (BELOW).

Non-pedigree cats come in a multitude of colours, fur lengths and coat patterns. Sleek black cats **(RIGHT)** *are always popular and highly sought-after, while this little odd-eyed white, auburn and tortie kitten* **(OPPOSITE)** *has instant appeal.*

*Kittens develop quickly and even within a few weeks look quite different. At eight weeks old (**RIGHT**), the soft, fluffy kitten coat and babyish expression is apparent, but only four weeks later (**FAR RIGHT**) the kitten looks far more like a small version of the adult cat it will become. At twelve weeks old the kitten is ready for its inoculations.*

many as there used to be. Some rescue organisations now offer subsidized neutering through a local vet and, in some cases, may even pay the whole bill. These schemes have been devised to try and control the population of unwanted cats, and in consequence there are fewer moggie kittens available to the responsible buyer. Other good sources are local papers which carry a 'pets for sale' column, and local cat clubs and cat charities which will also know of any kittens needing a home, as will most veterinary practices.

The age at which a non-pedigree cat goes to its new home will vary, but should certainly never be less than eight weeks. By this time the kitten, although not completely self-sufficient, is old enough to stand on its own four paws. But it will no longer have the immunity to infections that it received while suckling its mother's milk, as this contained protective antibodies, so from the age of six weeks the kitten is at its most vulnerable as it has no protection from disease, and twelve weeks is the earliest age that most veterinarians will administer the all important inoculations. However, it is reasonably safe to allow an eight-week-old to go to a new home that does not have any cats or dogs already, as long as the

kitten can be confined indoors until it is old enough for its first shots. If this is not practicable, it should stay with its mother until twelve weeks old.

◆ PEDIGREE KITTENS ◆

Pedigree cats are expensive, and not without reason. The cost of buying a pedigree female cat of suitable quality and the cost of the stud fee are only the first of many expenses (*see 'Breeding From Your Cat'*).

There are more than one hundred breeds to choose from, including the different coat colours and patterns within each breed. If you do not have a firm idea about the breed you would like, look

BELOW
It is not just rescued 'moggies' that are looking for homes; most cat breed clubs will have adult cats of your chosen breed needing homes too.

● RESCUE CENTRES ●

There are so many unwanted cats in need of good homes that it makes sense to take one from a rescue centre. It is not just moggies that are looking for homes. In the UK, all breed clubs affiliated to the Governing Council of the Cat Fancy (GCCF) have an appointed welfare officer in charge of rehoming, so if a particular pedigree breed is your preference, contact the club for that breed. No such equivalent is available in the USA, although a club will probably be able to advise you. If you decide to adopt a rescue, be prepared to go through the third degree by way of interrogation. No responsible rehoming service will allow a cat to leave the premises unless the officer is absolutely sure that the cat is going to have a home for the rest of its life and will not become a rehomer again in a few weeks' time. It may seem as if you are being interviewed as stringently as if you were adopting a baby. The officer may even make a visit to your home to ensure it is suitable, and follow up in a few weeks' time to check that the cat has settled well with the family.

All rescue work relies on charitable donation, so be prepared to put your hand in your pocket. Any cat taken as a rescue will have been thoroughly checked over by a veterinarian, have been neutered, and have received the necessary inoculations. This all costs money. A good permanent home for the cat is the main priority, but if you are able to afford a donation, do so.

Rescue centres often have a multitude of pretty, healthy cats ready for adoption (ABOVE). This beautiful, albeit one-eyed, cat (LEFT) started life with a deprived kittenhood. Neglected and unwanted, she succumbed to cat flu, causing ulceration to one eye which had to be removed. Months on, with much loving care and the correct veterinary treatment, she is a cat that her new owner is justifiably proud of.

LEFT
A visit to a cat show will provide the opportunity to see many different breeds and to meet the owners and breeders; most are very helpful and will outline the finer points of their particular breed to aid you with your decision.

through some cat-breed guides in the library. Each breed is intrinsically different, not just in appearance, but in character, too. Even within the breeds, some colour variations have slightly different temperaments. Having read about all the different varieties – and do remember that not all breeds of cat are available in every country – the next thing to do is meet up with the cats 'in the fur'. A visit to an all-breed cat show will give you the opportunity to see as many breeds as possible.

At the show, you will probably decide on the breed that most suits you. In the USA, you can buy cats direct from a show. In the UK, however, cat shows are only a shop window; you are not allowed to actually buy. But you will probably meet breeders of the types of cat that interest you. If not, you may know someone with a cat of the same breed, who can advise you of a reputable breeder. If this is not possible, contact the appropriate breed club, which will run a list of kittens available and so should be able to put you in contact with a local breeder

(the appropriate governing body can provide you with this information). Specialist cat magazines carry advertisements of pedigree kittens for sale, as do local newspapers. Bear in mind that some breeds are rarer than others, and so you may have to wait several months for a kitten and even travel some distance to see the litter. Remember that cats at shows will not always act as they do at home, so it is very important to visit a breeder to see what the character of your preferred breed is like in a domestic environment before making a firm decision.

Arrange to visit only one cattery in a day, as it is easy to carry infections from one household of kittens to another. When you first contact the breeder, telephone for an appointment. You will probably be asked many questions at this point, but only to reassure both yourself and the breeder that you are not going to be wasting each other's time. Cat breeding is essentially a hobby, not a business; most breeders have a home, family and job to cope with as well as their cats and so are busier than most of us.

It is a politeness to let the breeder know just how many of you will be arriving on the appointed day, and if for any reason you are delayed, or unable to keep the appointment, telephone to say so. Try not to treat the occasion as a visit to the zoo and bring the whole family along – you are visiting a stranger's home. For the first visit, you and your partner are quite enough; leave any children behind. Never outstay your welcome, and although there will be many questions to be asked, try to keep them to

BELOW
*When visiting a
breeder, it is usual to
be able to see the
mother cat with her
kittens. However, you
may not be invited to
handle very young
kittens that have not
been inoculated and
are vulnerable to
infection.*

RIGHT
*These kittens have been
brought up in the
breeder's home and are
used to all the usual
household
accoutrements. If
raised in an outside
cattery, a young kitten
may take considerable
time to settle into a
domestic environment.*

*Although imperceptible to the novice pet owner, there are many subtle differences between a show-stopper and a pet-quality kitten, although to all intents and purposes the kitten will display most of the characteristics typical for the breed. This chinchilla (**LEFT**) shows the correct shape, colour and length of fur but the ears are too large and the nose too long. This kitten of the same breed (**BELOW RIGHT**) is destined for success on the show bench. Minor differences, but ones that a judge would take into serious consideration.*

a minimum. If you are serious about buying a kitten, there will be plenty of opportunity to ask advice later. Realize that no reputable breeder would allow a kitten to go to a new home on the very first visit – this will be one of several more to come.

If, at this first meeting, there are kittens in the home, do not be put off if you are not allowed to handle them, or are asked to disinfect your hands. This is no reflection on your personal hygiene, but a simple precaution against infection. However, you will be able to assess the general condition of the cats and kittens, and decide if this is going to be the breeder of your choice. You will most likely be asked to think it over for a week before making a final decision. Then, the breeder will invite you back, this time to meet any other members of your family, including children. Some young children are excellent with cats but others, especially those who have never shared their home with a cat before, may treat kittens like toys and be too rough with them. Many small children are especially fascinated by eyes and could easily accidentally poke a kitten's eye and damage it.

If children are too boisterous, do not be offended if the breeder refuses to sell you a kitten; wait a year or two until the children are old enough to realize that each cat is a living creature with its own personality, and so needs to be treated with the respect it deserves.

If all goes well, you will probably be asked for a deposit against the cost of the kitten. This works both ways: you are now assured that your kitten is definitely booked for you, and the breeder knows that your intentions are honourable. Deposits are returnable for good reasons such as illness or change of circumstance, but if you change your mind on a whim, do not expect to get your money back. The kitten has been reserved for you and if this commitment is not honoured the breeder has the added expense of keeping the kitten for longer, and maybe of readvertising it.

From the beginning, it is important to tell the breeder the reason for buying a kitten: is it purely as a pet, or do you wish to show or maybe even breed from it? No breeder would wish to see an example of their breeding exhibited on the show bench if it is not up to standard, as it would reflect on them and their breeding programme. In the UK, it is likely that those kittens unsuitable for breeding will have been placed on the non-active register, as this precludes breeding without the breeders' written consent to the GCCF. In the USA, there is no non-active register, however 'not for breeding' can be noted on the blue slip, or cats can be registered as neuters or spays after the relevant operation.

A pet-quality kitten of your chosen breed will be just the same as one sold for show and breeding, but may have some small fault, such as a tail kink or slightly misaligned jaw that would cause a show judge to withhold a prize. These are traits that you would not want to perpetuate through breeding.

All kittens have cost the same amount to raise, so many breeders will charge the same for pet-quality kittens as they do for those designated for the show bench or a breeding programme. Others differentiate, and charge more for show and breeding kittens than pets. At the end of the day, all cats should also be pets and, if you happen to enjoy going to shows, then this is an added bonus – the character and temperament of the cat will be the same regardless of the finer breed requisites laid down in the standard of points.

When you come to collect your kitten it should be at least twelve weeks old, wormed and fully inoculated. Make sure that you bring a sturdy cat carrier with you. It will probably be the first time the kitten has had to travel in a car, bus or

train and this can be a frightening experience, so it will feel much more secure if contained in a carrier.

Before leaving, the breeder should provide you with:

- Inoculation certificate
- Pedigree of at least four generations
- Transfer form
- Diet sheet, outlining the types of food the kitten is used to and times of feeding

WHAT TO LOOK FOR IN A KITTEN

W hatever your preference, pedigree or non-pedigree, the kitten should be fit, healthy, happy and friendly.

The main difference between pedigree and non-pedigree cats is that you know the parentage of pedigrees. To a certain extent, health and temperament can be inherited; if you know who the mother and father are, and have met them, you will have a fair idea of the character your kitten will have when it grows up. All

BELOW

If purchasing a pedigree cat you will have probably visited the kitten at the breeder's home and met its parents. Many characteristics are genetically based, so if your kitten's parents are healthy and sweet-tempered, it is likely their offspring will exhibit the same traits.

ABOVE

When collecting your new kitten from the breeder, do ensure that you take a safe cat carrier with you so the kitten feels secure during the journey to its new home.

◈ SIMPLE HEALTH CHECKS ◈

1 The ears should be clean and free from parasites.

2 The eyes should be clear and bright, without any trace of debris in the corners.

3 The mouth and gums should have a healthy pink tinge.

4 For a show specimen, the tail should be straight without any sign of a kink.

5 The coat should be clean and clear of parasites.

6 The anal region should be clean with no trace of faecal matter.

7 The tummy should feel full and soft; any hardness in this region could denote the presence of worm infestation.

ABOVE

Be wary of accepting a cat that appears frightened of humans. Unused to domestic home life, it will take a long time to adjust to a new home and will require many patient hours of tender loving care to settle in.

kittens should be used to the usual household hubbub: the sounds of dishwashers, washing machines, vacuum cleaners and television sets should not frighten them.

Be wary of buying a kitten that has been brought up outside in a cattery, as it may take a long time to settle into the alien environment of a normal home. Try to get your kitten from a similar family situation to your own; for example, if you already have a dog, find a kitten that has been brought up with dogs and is used to them. The same goes for households with children and babies. It is traumatic enough for a kitten to be moved to a different home, without having strange new creatures to contend with too.

Here are some indications to health and temperament you should look out for:

◗ Kittens should be used to being handled from birth, and should not be frightened of humans.

◗ If the kitten hisses or spits at you, or seems timid and nervous, you are better off looking elsewhere for your pet.

◗ The kittens should all have bright eyes and clean coats with no sign of parasitic infestation.

◗ Their tummies should feel plump but soft; any hardness could indicate worm infestation.

◗ The ears, too, should be clean; any brown, waxy deposits may mean the kitten has ear mites.

◗ Look at the kittens' litter tray: is it clean, too? A strong smell along with runny excrement could indicate some infection.

SETTLING YOUR ◗ CAT OR KITTEN ◗ INTO ITS NEW HOME

Before you collect your cat or kitten, make sure that you have all the necessary equipment. Do not leave this until the last minute, or you may find the shops shut: washing up bowls and roasting trays prove expensive alternatives to a litter tray, although they serve in an emergency.

The basic items needed to start with are:

◗ Litter tray
◗ Cat litter and litter scoop
◗ Food and water bowls
◗ Food
◗ Sleeping basket and bedding
◗ Cat carrier
◗ Scratching post and toys
◗ Collar and tag

The best time to introduce a cat into your home is when you have plenty of time to spare, and there are few other people

Continued page 41

ABOVE

Separate food and water bowls are a must; the plastic variety is probably the most useful.

ABOVE

A litter tray will be needed if the cat is not allowed outside; covered trays prevent cat litter being scattered over the floor.

ABOVE

A collar is essential if the cat is to be allowed outdoors.

ABOVE

A cat should be provided with its own bed, and this heated one would fit the bill nicely.

BELOW

For visits to the vet, or the boarding cattery, a sturdy cat carrier will be needed.

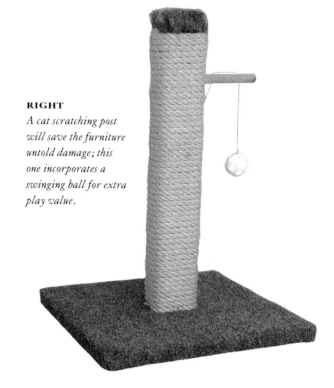

RIGHT

A cat scratching post will save the furniture untold damage; this one incorporates a swinging ball for extra play value.

KITTENS AND PLAY

BELOW
Toys scented with catnip or cat mint often bring out the wild streak in a domestic kitten.

ABOVE
A 'spider' toy made of a ball of wool and pipe cleaners is being cautiously inspected. A tug on the string, causing the toy to move, will probably incite the predatory instincts of a kitten. A toy such as this should only be offered for play under strict supervision as the pipe cleaners contain wire which, if chewed, might harm a kitten.

Kittens love to play and this provides much more than just simple pleasure to a young developing cat. Play involves the use of all the muscles in the body, and aids strong, healthy growth and development. Two kittens will happily play together and this encourages social development too; they will also enjoy the added stimulus of toys to play with. A sole kitten actually *needs* toys if it is to develop, both socially and physically, into a healthy, well-adjusted adult.

A play pole, covered in rope or similar fabric, will encourage the kitten to scratch. This saves both your carpets and furnishings, and provides a most necessary function; the kitten will both clean and sharpen its claws while scratching. This action exercises not only the claws and paws, but also extends to the muscles

in the legs and the back, and so is of great importance to the cat's general wellbeing. Moreover, this is why any owner should think twice about de-clawing, a deplorable operation that, fortunately, is prohibited in the UK.

Toys, especially those scented with cat mint, will also cause great excitement and interest, and ensures that the olfactory lobes are exercised too. In addition, they will stimulate a kitten confined to a domestic environment to simulate the natural responses it would have when catching prey. Noisy toys will cause interest, too, whether they be by way of a squeak or a rattle! This all helps to keep the ear senses well tuned.

Just as with a small child, toys provide much, much more than mere fun – they are part of the process of not just learning, but also of growing up.

BELOW
*A play pole with toys
suspended from it will
encourage a young cat
to play, exercise and
scratch – activities
vital to a cat's
wellbeing.*

TOP AND ABOVE
*Kittens, like children,
often discover a play
value in toys other
than those intended.
This toy incorporates a
catnip-scented ball and
is designed to
encourage the kitten to
pat it back and forth
on its flexible stalk.
This contrary kitten,
however, is
determined to wrestle
the stalk from its
fixing.*

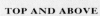

RIGHT
If you have chosen an adult cat, you will need to give it a lot of time and attention to help it settle into a new domestic environment.

BELOW
Cats and children can make ideal sleeping companions. But remember, this will be a hard habit to break and the cat will expect to sleep in the bed for the rest of its life.

around. Most kittens settle in quickly but it may take a little while to introduce an adult cat to new surroundings. If you are at work during the day, try to take a few days off either side of the weekend so that you and your new cat have some time to spend together. If you have children, it may be better to get the kitten accustomed to your home while they are at school.

Before the cat arrives, decide the most suitable sites for the litter tray and feeding bowls. Let the cat see these as soon as it arrives – it may need the litter tray immediately; accidents will happen and the stress of travelling from one home to another can play havoc on the bowels!

Also, think about the cat's sleeping arrangements. Cats like to sleep in the warmest part of the house, and they like company too, so given the choice your new cat will opt to sleep in bed with you. Old habits die hard; you may be tempted to allow your kitten to sleep with you for the first night or two, but it will be hard to persuade it a few weeks later that these

BELOW
Cat beds come in many shapes and sizes and many cats find an 'igloo' most acceptable. Site the bed in a fairly warm room.

ABOVE
Make sure that you site the litter tray in a place convenient for both your cat and family and leave it there. The cat will become understandably confused if the tray is moved to a different location in the house.

ABOVE

Cats are natural escape artists, and if they know something interesting lies on the other side of a door, they will make every attempt to get out.

are not its designated sleeping quarters, and you may find yourself with a furry sleeping partner for life. If you do not want to share your bed with your cat, make this quite clear from the outset. Make a cosy nest for your kitten in its own basket; put in suitable bedding materials, a hot water bottle and some toys; place the basket in a warm spot in the room you feel is best for the cat's night-time accommodation – and keep your bedroom door shut.

Cats do not like unnecessary upheaval. When they know exactly where they can find their food, litter tray and bed, stay with this arrangement. Never lock the cat out of the room that contains the litter tray, or you may find a mess to clear up in the morning.

Gradually introduce your cat to those areas of your home that you are going to give it access to. You may prefer to keep

some rooms cat-free, so make this clear from the beginning by keeping the doors closed. Once a cat has been inside a room, and later finds the door locked, it will be forever miaowing to get back in, or scratching at the carpet.

The main place your cat or kitten will inhabit is the living room as this is the area most used by you and your family, so let this be its first room to explore. Remember that your home is alien territory to a kitten and it may be quite frightened by suddenly being exposed to a large house with lots of rooms. Introducing an adult cat, neutered or not, to new surroundings may well evoke territorial behaviour such as spraying, which can be difficult to cure.

Whether you have opted for an adult cat or a kitten, introduce it to your home room by room over a period of several days. As the cat becomes more confident of the layout of the house, it can be left to wander freely indoors.

Do be careful to keep the cat inside for at least a week, even if eventually you are going to allow it free access to your garden. Cats are great escapologists, so keep the front and back doors shut, and make sure that the windows are closed too. It is surprising how small a gap a cat can crawl through and, if it does get out, it may panic in new surroundings and get lost or, worse still, run over.

INTRODUCING YOUR CAT TO OTHER ANIMALS IN THE HOME

Your new cat or kitten will probably be the centre of attention when you first bring it home, but do not exclude any existing pets from your attentions as this will make them very jealous of the new intruder and may prolong the settling process. Make sure that both animals get the same amount of attention.

If you already own an adult cat and want to introduce another, it can take

RIGHT
*Finding the door
firmly shut, this cat
has jumped onto a
suitable work surface
and, undaunted, starts
to paw at the bolt.*

LEFT
*Having achieved its
purpose, the cat is now
free to explore the
great wide yonder. If
you want to prohibit
your cat from
roaming, outside or
within the house, keep
all doors and windows
firmly shut.*

◉ CATS AND CHILDREN ◉

If you have children, explain to them that the new cat is not a furry toy. Children are usually good with animals, but some can be a little over-enthusiastic and excited. Teach children the correct way to hold a cat; explain that tails are not designed to be pulled and that the creature should be treated with respect. Your children will love to play with the kitten, but make sure that they do not get too rough with it; young bones are delicate and can easily be broken. Remember, too, that cats have a very good self-defence system; if your child gets too rumbustious, the cat will quite likely use its claws and there

A single cat and an only child (BELOW) **can be devoted companions.**

will be tears before bedtime. To prevent eye injuries, teach children not to push their faces up close to the cat. This is also the time to teach children to adopt the sensible hygiene practice of washing hands after handling animals, particularly before meals, and always after carrying out of litter tray duties.

Most of all this is common sense. Take plenty of time with your new cat, introducing it gradually to its new home, and you should find that you have a happy, contented and sociable pet for many years to come.

Children should be taught the correct way to handle a cat and this little girl (ABOVE) **has got it all right.**

Cats love to be part of the family but a brief instruction from mother to a young child will ensure that they all live in harmony (RIGHT).

BELOW
An established pet and a cat new to the household can, with sensitive handling, become the best of friends as this huge, solid ginger-and-white moggie boy and elegant, slender Siamese girl demonstrate.

LEFT
Cats that have been brought up together since kittenhood invariably get on well together, even if not of the same litter.

quite a time to get them to settle down together. The resident cat will not appreciate the newcomer at first and, if you are not careful, there will be a lot of caterwauling and fur flying. Introductions must be done gradually.

Smell is very important to cats, so take a blanket or piece of fabric from your home and put it in the carrier you collect your new cat in. It will smell, not only of your house, but of the resident animals, and will give the cat a chance to sniff out the family before it gets home. It helps if the newcomer smells familiar too, so if you use perfume or cologne, rub a little on the new cat before you bring it into your home, and it will seem less of a threat to the resident feline. You could also try putting sardine or pilchard juice on each cat, which may seem strange, but the most important thing is for the cats to smell the same, and this idea might even get them to start washing each other.

Food is another good way to get cats to accept each other; feed them in the same room, from separate bowls. As the cats become engrossed in their meal, gradually move the bowls nearer together. When the meals are finished, the cats will invariably start to wash; the nearer together they are, the more likely they are to indulge in social grooming, a sure sign of feline acceptance.

When you sit down for the evening, make sure that each cat has a vacant lap on which to sit. If you live on your own, get a friend to drop by for a while. This ensures that both cats feel they are getting

the same amount of attention. Swap cats from time to time; in this way they will pick up each other's smells and be assured that the other cat is not a threat. Use similar tactics when introducing them to different rooms; one cat in one room, one in the other, and swap over after an hour or so. This gives each time to sniff out the opposition.

If you have a kitten pen, use it during this settling-in period. With one cat in the pen, and the other free to wander around the room, they will be able to look at each other, but if they do decide to have a confrontation, will not actually get close enough to cause harm.

It is much easier to settle a kitten with an adult than it is to introduce two grown-up cats. Most adult cats, even males, will show a kind of parental instinct to a small newcomer. All the above procedures apply to introducing a kitten, but it should take much less time for the two to accept each other.

ABOVE
A kitten pen is designed to keep small kittens away from harm. It can also be used to keep one cat away from another during the initial settling-in period.

● HOW TO HOLD A CAT ●

A cat should always be held in such a way that it feels secure. Gently cradle the back and rear quarters with one hand and support the shoulders with the other so the cat feels reassured that it is in safe hands.

Introducing your cat or kitten to the family dog should be treated with caution. If the kitten has grown up with a dog, and your dog is used to cats, there should be few problems. If not, tread very carefully. Some breeds of dog, such as many of the terrier varieties, are instinctive 'ratters' and may react to a kitten as they would to a rabbit. Again, if you have one, use a kitten pen so that the dog and cat can see and smell each other without the risk of either being hurt. If there is a fight, it is quite likely that the dog will come off worse: cats are extremely agile, move quickly, can jump and have sharp claws.

Whichever animals you are introducing – cats, kittens or dogs – it is *most important* that they are not left unsupervised until you are completely satisfied that they have integrated. In the meantime, put them in separate rooms and shut the doors firmly whenever you have to leave the house.

ABOVE AND RIGHT
Introducing a strange dog and cat to each other should only be done under supervision. Despite the difference in size it is more likely that the dog will come off the worse for wear. After an initial sniff these two were soon on hugging terms.

CARING FOR YOUR CAT

When you first bring your new cat or kitten home it should already have been inoculated, wormed and checked over by a veterinary surgeon for general health. Now it is your duty to keep the cat fit and healthy; routine maintenance, and a balanced diet, are the basis of this.

CHOOSING A VETERINARY SURGEON

The first priority is to find a veterinary surgeon, and to register with the practice. Do not wait until your cat is ill, or has had some accident; you never know when your cat might need medical attention, and if you and your cat are already known to a vet, he or she will have all the background information.

Although all vets are GPs, and have a broad knowledge of all animals, some practices are specifically for domestic pets. These are found mainly in large towns and cities, where most of the patients are cats and dogs. In the country, especially in farming communities, most vets will be more used to dealing with large animals, such as sheep and cattle. It is important to find a vet who has a good knowledge of cats, and is up to date on the various illnesses and ailments that can affect the feline, along with their appropriate treatment. Some years ago, a cat breeder friend of mine moved from a city environment to a remote country area. When she approached the local vet to have a litter of kittens inoculated, he shook his head in bewilderment. He was used to servicing the local farming community, who thought of cats as mousers, and would not dream of spending their hard-earned money on inoculating them. Having never been asked for such a service before, he did not carry any vaccine in stock; it took over a week to order it and cost considerably more than my friend was used to paying.

Nonetheless, it is useful to find a vet locally; it is pointless to register with the best cat practice in the country if it is going to take several hours to travel there. If you have bought your kitten from a local breeder, or obtained a cat from a local rescue centre, ask them to recommend a vet. Ask local cat owners, too, which practice they go to. Some of the larger cat clubs have local advisers who may be able to help you. Personal recommendation is always best, but if this fails, look through the commercial pages of the phone book; this will list all the veterinary practices.

When you have selected a veterinary surgeon, telephone the practice and make an appointment to meet. Ask if the vet would like to meet your cat too; after all this is who will be the patient. It is important for you to feel confident in your vet's abilities and approach. If all seems well, and the three of you get along together, register the cat there. Make sure that you take the inoculation certificate with you, as the vet will need to log this information in order to remind you when the annual booster shot is due.

BELOW
When the annual booster inoculation is due, ask the vet to give your cat a thorough health check at the same time.

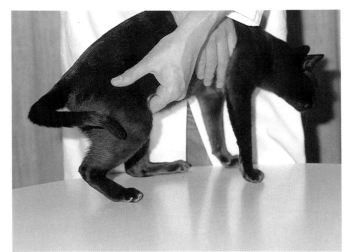

ABOVE
Cat owners should register their feline charges with a local veterinary practice as soon as possible, and not just when treatment is needed. Even with minor ailments it is important to visit the vet for a correct diagnosis, a prescription, if necessary, and advice for the correct administration of any medication, such as eye ointment. Never apply or administer any kind of medicinal preparation developed for human use.

ROUTINE CARE

Apart from supplying your cat with a balanced diet (*see 'Feeding Your Cat'*) there are other little things you can do to help it stay fit and healthy.

Regular grooming (*see 'Grooming Your Cat'*) will help keep the cat's coat sparkling and free of tangles, and will help to stop fur balls forming. You will also be able to spot any sign of fleas, or other external parasites, and treat them before they become a problem. In the same way, you will see any telltale signs of tapeworm infestation (*see 'Parasites'*).

Claws, eyes, ears and teeth all benefit from regular examination. Try to make this a regular routine, perhaps every fortnight or so. Once the cat is accustomed to the idea, it will probably start to enjoy these little sessions.

◆ CLAWS ◆

Clipping your cat's claws will save your furniture and, possibly yourself, from damage. Cats that go outside will naturally strop tree trunks to keep their claws to a manageable length. Pro-

LEFT
If a cat is allowed outside it will use tree trunks or wooden posts for stropping, thereby preventing its claws from growing too long.

LEFT
A cat scratching post, with playthings attached, will give your cat hours of pleasure with the added bonus of saving the furniture and carpets from its sharp claws.

viding a scratching post in your home will satisfy an indoor cat's need to scratch to a certain extent. A word of warning: never cover the scratching post with the same carpet as that which furnishes your home; this may look aesthetically pleasing, but will confuse the cat, who will think the carpet is an extension of the post, and will scratch that too.

Clipping claws should be done with care, and it is best to get your vet to show you how to do this the first time. Holding the cat firmly (you may need a friend to help), push the paw pad of each individual claw inward, one at a time; this will reveal the unsheathed claw. You will now see two quite different colours to the claw, a pink area in the middle, surrounded by a whitish covering culminating in the pointed end of the claw. The pink area contains the blood supply and the nerves and, if cut, would cause pain and bleeding. The sharp, white point of the claw is composed only of dead cells, and is perfectly safe to cut. Special claw clippers can be bought from the pet store, but ordinary nail clippers designed for humans are just as effective, and a lot cheaper. Your cat may object to claw cutting at first but, once introduced to the routine, it will soon accept a fortnightly clipping session.

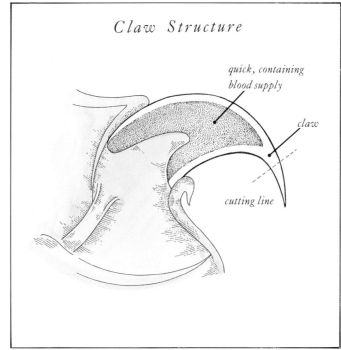

Claw Structure

quick, containing
blood supply

claw

cutting line

*If your cat is to be confined indoors without access to trees where it could naturally strop its claws, it is a wise precaution to blunt the tips of the claws to remove the sharp point. This can be done with ordinary toenail clippers (**ABOVE**) or with specialized feline claw clippers (**RIGHT**). See the diagram (**ABOVE RIGHT**) before attempting to do this; ascertaining the correct cutting line is vitally important to prevent injury.*

RIGHT
The nictitating membrane or haw (the third eyelid) is not usually visible in a healthy cat; when it is apparent it can be indicative of ill-health. However, in paler coloured Siamese it is not unusual for a small amount of haw to show even though the cat is in perfect condition.

BELOW
Any 'sleep' left deposited in the corner of the eye can be removed gently with a piece of moistened cotton wool.

◦ EYES ◦

It is not unusual to find small deposits of matter in the corner of the eye; this can be removed with some cotton wool moistened with cooled boiled water or, if you are careful, with your clean little finger – but be careful not to poke the cat in the eye. The third eyelid (haw or nictitating membrane) should not be visible in a healthy cat.

The cat is unusual in that it has three eyelids, two of which move up and down like our own. The haw moves across the eye from the side nearest the nose towards the outer edge. If dust, or even cat litter, gets in your cat's eye, it will cause the haw to come up – if this is the case, bathing the eye in a little dilute eye wash will have a soothing effect. However, a visible haw can be an early warning of impending illness and, if it is still up after twenty-

four hours, you should consult the vet. A rough guideline: if only one haw is up the chances are that there is a foreign body in the eye, but if both are up it is likely that the cat is unwell.

If the cat seems to have runny eyes, especially if accompanied by sneezing, it may be sickening for cat flu. Or it could be suffering an allergic reaction.

ABOVE

Ears can be cleaned with either moistened cotton wool or, with care, a cotton bud but be sure never to delve too deep into the ear canal.

EARS

The ears should smell and look clean, with no sign of waxy build-up. The pinna, or exterior ear, can be cleaned with a little moistened cotton wool or, very carefully, with a cotton bud. Never delve deep into the ear canal, as this could cause damage. Any brown, waxy debris may indicate ear mite infestation and, if this is suspected, it should be diagnosed and treated by your vet.

TEETH

The teeth should look clean, and the breath smell sweet. Diet (*see 'Feeding Your Cat'*) is very important for the development of healthy teeth in early years. In order to keep gums healthy, and to prevent the build-up of tartar and plaque, your cat should always be given something to chew on such as a non-splintering bone, dried meat or certain suitable dried biscuits. If your cat persistently scratches at its face, or refuses to eat, it may have a loose tooth, gingivitis (gum inflammation) or both. Contact the vet immediately as an extraction and treatment may be needed.

OTHER POINTS TO CHECK

Always look out for any unusual lump or bump. This may be a simple sebaceous cyst; it could also be the start of a tumour. Any change in temperament could indicate injury or illness.

It cannot be stressed enough how important regular observation and examination of your cat is. Remember that your vet will usually only see your cat once a year for the annual check-up and boosters. You know your cat best as it lives with you twenty-four hours a day and so you are the person who will notice if the cat is 'not quite right'. Do not be afraid to mention the smallest change in your cat's shape, size, personality or behaviour to your vet; what may seem trivial to you could be vital information that will help provide a correct diagnosis.

ABOVE

Regular examination of your cat's mouth will give you an indication of any impending problems. Look out for inflamed gums or loose teeth and if this is the case contact your vet immediately.

FEEDING YOUR CAT

A proper, well-balanced diet is of paramount importance to the health and wellbeing of your cat. Food is not just a fuel to keep the body ticking over; it directly affects the condition of your cat's teeth and bones, all the internal organs, especially the bowels, and ultimately the chosen diet will be reflected in the condition of the cat's coat.

No matter where you have acquired your cat, it should be in the peak of condition when you accept it into your home. If you bought a kitten from a breeder, you should have been given a diet sheet to help it through the first few months. Cat or kitten, you have taken on responsibility for its welfare, and nothing is more important than correct feeding.

Cats are creatures of habit and so it is important, right from the start, to implement a regime for feeding times and the location of food and water bowls. The diet that the cat requires will vary according to its age. A kitten needs feeding little and often, and the same applies to an older cat. A healthy adult cat needs fewer

but larger meals. An invalid cat may require a special diet and your vet will advise you on this.

EQUIPMENT AND WHERE TO PUT IT

M ost owners find that the kitchen is the most convenient place to feed their cat, as this is where food is stored and prepared. It is probably not a good

BELOW
Feeding bowls: (from left to right) time-controlled, glass, metal, earthenware, plastic, double-bowl. There are advantages, and some disadvantages, with each of these types. Select bowls that work for you and are acceptable to your cat.

ABOVE
To avoid forever tripping over food and water bowls, consider feeding your cat on a free work surface in the kitchen.

Product cat food: (clockwise from 11 o'clock) dried biscuits, semi-moist 'nuggets', canned food, vacuum-sealed punnet, dried protein diet. All these foods provide nutrition, but for a well-balanced and pleasing diet offer your cat a selection of these prepared foods and fresh food.

idea to feed the cat on the floor, as you will be forever tripping over the bowls. A tray containing the food and water bowls placed on a spare work surface keeps everything in one place and out of the way. If you have a utility room, this may be more convenient. Once established, keep to the routine; your cat needs to have permanent access to fresh water and so needs to know where to find the water bowl.

Bowls

There are many different kinds of food bowl available, some better and more practical than others.

PLASTIC bowls are probably the most common as they are durable, almost un-breakable and easy to clean. Not all are dishwasher-proof.

METAL bowls are indestructible and can be sterilized at a high temperature with-out damage.

EARTHENWARE bowls are solid and will not tip over easily but are easily broken or chipped if dropped.

GLASS bowls are not a good idea; they may look pretty, but if dropped they will break with the risk that fragments of

glass will get embedded in the cat's paws or, worse still, be swallowed.

DOUBLE BOWLS which can hold both food and water look like a good idea; however, if the water needs changing before the cat has finished all the food, it is almost impossible to empty the water without spilling the food.

TIME-CONTROLLED feeding bowls can be a boon to anyone who is out at work all day. These consist of two removable bowls inside a lidded container with a programmable timer. You set the time that the cat should be fed, and the lid pops up to allow the cat to get to its food. In hot countries, this has the added bonus that it keeps flies off the food. One drawback: some cats do not take long to realize how the time control works!

◆ CHOICE OF FOOD ◆

Cats are natural carnivores and a look at their teeth will confirm this: large canines to tear flesh; tiny incisors as the cat has little need to nibble at grass and vegetation; and a hefty set of molars to aid chewing. In the wild, a cat catches prey and eats it whole: feathers, fur, bones and, quite importantly, the content of the stomach and bowels; this last item is

CANNED FOOD is probably the most popular. It is convenient, easy to store, and should contain a perfect balance of nutrients, vitamins and minerals essential for a cat's wellbeing. Some brands have a special kitten formula, especially designed for the dietary needs of a younger cat. Canned foods are available in many different flavours, so your cat will always have variety. One reservation – some cats find that certain brands of canned food are too rich and can cause diarrhoea.

BISCUITS provide an interesting and crunchy supplement to your cat's diet, but should never be used as the sole food supply. A few sprinkled on your cat's usual food will provide exercise for the jaws and help keep the teeth and gums healthy.

DRIED PROTEIN diets are a recent development. They are based on scientific principles and are usually formulated from hydrolysed beef protein. They are the ultimate complete balanced diet, and contain every possible vitamin, mineral and trace element a cat needs. They are easy to store, convenient to serve, and have the bonus that they can be left down when you are out and will not spoil like canned food. There are special kinds available, such as formulas for kittens and 'less active' cats.

SEMI-MOIST 'NUGGETS' in vacuum-sealed pouches are a food many cats find irresistible. They are easy to store and, once opened, do not deteriorate as fast as the canned varieties. They make an excellent 'treat' for your cat, but should not form the main constituent of its diet.

VACUUM-SEALED PUNNETS are another new kind of food containing fresh-cooked fish, meat or chicken. These contain no preservatives or colouring and so are especially suitable for cats with delicate stomachs.

FRESH FOOD should, ideally, be offered for one of the meals each day. It could be cooked, filleted chicken, rabbit or fish, but be sure that all bones are removed, as

ABOVE
Some breeds of cat have a greater predilection to obesity than others. British Shorthairs fall into this category and their diet should be carefully monitored, especially if the cat is a less active neuter.

usually vegetable matter which provides trace elements the cat would not otherwise have access to.

In modern society, we tend to frown on cats catching birds and mice; it is a messy business and opening a tin or packet seems a more hygienic way to provide the cat with its basic dietary needs. The key to providing a good diet is balance, so consider all the different varieties available.

There are so many kinds of cat food on the market that both you and your cat will be spoiled for choice. Variety is the spice of life; by feeding your cat a combination of some of the different foods available, you will ensure an interesting, balanced and adequate diet.

they could easily get stuck in the throat. Almost all cats enjoy cooked meats such as beef and lamb. Some prefer raw food, and for them, a little raw, lean beef will be greeted with enthusiasm – it is unwise to give your cat raw fish, chicken or other kinds of meat. If you are feeding fresh food, do make sure that you buy 'human consumption' quality; some butchers sell 'pet mince' which is made from fatty beef and, although suitable for dogs, can cause digestive problems in cats.

TABLE SCRAPS are often fed to cats and can provide a valuable extra source of nutrition. Vegetables, especially greens, are particularly useful, as they echo the natural diet of a cat in the wild. Cooked meat bones – not chicken or rabbit – will give the cat something to chew on. Never offer a cat bones that might splinter, but leftovers from the roast joint, or chops, will give the cat hours of pleasure and will also help keep the teeth and gums exercised and healthy.

VITAMIN AND MINERAL SUPPLEMENTS can be bought at most pet stores. Read the instructions on the container thoroughly, as it is possible to overdose your cat on some supplements. If you feel that your cat is lacking some vital mineral or vitamin, consult your vet.

FEEDING: HOW MUCH AND HOW OFTEN

The average adult, neutered cat needs two meals each day. The amount of food needed depends on the size and build of the cat. As a rough guideline, 250 grams (8 oz) of canned cat food per meal (one small can, or half of a large can) is enough. This is roughly equivalent to a 100-gram (3-oz) portion of freshly cooked fish or chicken.

After the first six to nine months, kittens need a similar amount of food to adult cats, but it should spread over four meals a day; the same goes for older 'senior citizen' cats – little and often is the right approach.

Pregnant or lactating queens, and working stud cats, need a different diet with vitamin and mineral supplements (*see 'Breeding From Your Cat'*).

Although obese cats are sometimes seen, they are not very common. Cats are usually sensible about their waistlines, and tend not to overindulge. However, some cats, and some breeds in particular, are prone to becoming overweight. As a conscientious cat owner, you will know if your cat is becoming too fat; if you are in doubt contact your vet for advice. Personally, I feel that it is better for a cat to be slightly plump than verging on the anorexic; if it then suffers a slight illness, and does not feed for a while, it has some substance to fall back on.

ABOVE
Encouraging cats at a young age to chew meat from the bone will help the teeth to become stronger and less likely to decay in old age.

GROOMING YOUR CAT

Cats are fastidious animals, and usually manage to keep their fur coats in pristine order. However, as with most things, a little help from a friend does not go amiss; when several cats live together they will indulge in social grooming, and spend hours washing each other. Usually, they will pay special attention to those awkward places that a single cat cannot easily reach, such as behind the ears and the back of the neck.

This does not mean that a human friend cannot help out too; indeed, with our modern urban environment and centrally heated houses, it is important for all cats to have some extra grooming. Both longhaired and shorthaired cats moult; in the wild this would be confined to the warm summer months when the cat needed to shed some of its heavy, winter overcoat. In a home with a controlled temperature, cats moult a little all year round. When a cat grooms itself, a certain amount of fur is ingested, and this can lead to a build-up of fur balls in the stomach (*see Health Care, Ailments and Illnesses*). Regular grooming will help stop these forming.

Introduce your cat to regular grooming sessions as soon as possible; it is

ABOVE

The mother cat will spend many hours making sure her offspring are immaculately clean.

RIGHT

Social grooming is an important aspect of a cat's life – what better than a friend to help wash those inaccessible parts, such as behind the ears.

LEFT
*Even a solitary cat
will spend a large part
of its day attending to
matters of personal
hygiene. Despite this
predilection of the
species to personal and
social grooming, all
cats need a helping
hand from their
owners, too.*

always easier to get a young animal used to the routine than it is an older animal. From the cat's point of view, once it is used to them, these grooming sessions are thoroughly enjoyable: most cats love being stroked and touched, and a good brushing, combined with some hand grooming, can result in a feline drooling with pleasure.

GROOMING EQUIPMENT

When buying any grooming equipment, make sure that you buy from a reputable pet store. The cheapest equipment might seem like a bargain, but is not always the best. It probably will not last as long as a better-quality product and might even damage your cat. Ensure that any metal combs have *blunt*, *rounded* teeth, and that there are no sharp points.

The equipment you need depends on the length of the cat's coat. These are some of the most readily available:

For a shorthaired cat: chamois leather, bristle brush or baby brush, rubber grooming pad, flea comb, bay rum.

For a longhaired cat: wire and bristle double-sided brush, toothbrush, slicker brush, talcum powder, metal comb with alternate long/short teeth, wide-toothed comb.

LEFT
*Here is a range of
grooming equipment
needed for a
shorthaired cat (items
on left of picture), and
a longhaired cat (items
to right) as detailed
above.*

STEP-BY-STEP TO GROOMING A SHORTHAIR CAT

Shorthairs, on the whole, do not need a tremendous amount of grooming, but still benefit from a regular brush and comb to help remove dead or loose hairs. A polish with chamois leather will also impart a glossy sheen. Some pedigree breeds, such as British Shorthairs and Manx, have particularly thick coats and so special attention needs to be paid to any early signs of a mat forming.

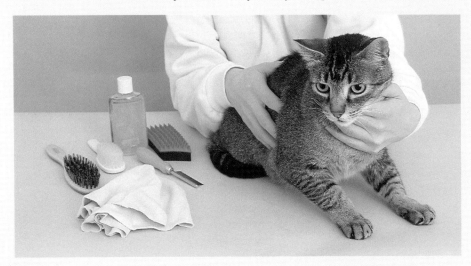

1 For a shorthair cat you will need: (clockwise from top) bay rum, rubber grooming pad, flea comb, chamois leather, bristle or baby brush.

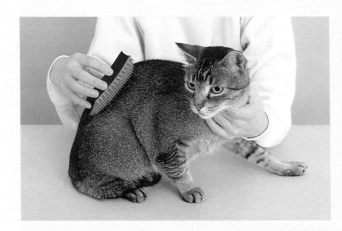

2 A special rubber pad is used to loosen up any dead hairs. The studded surface collects most of the excess fur and provides the added benefit of giving the cat a pleasant massage to stimulate the circulation. It is important not to overdo this first stage as the pad is extremely effective and an over-enthusiastic owner can loosen too much fur. These pads are available in most good pet stores but if it is difficult to find one, try using damp hands as a substitute.

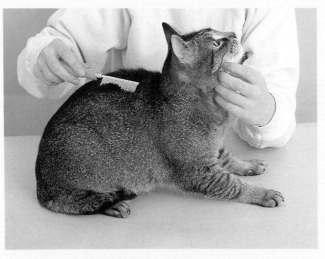

3 Use a fine-toothed comb (usually called a flea comb, but not necessarily used for removing fleas) to comb the coat gently in the opposite direction to that in which it naturally lies; this ensures that the deep-lying dead fur is removed. Then comb thoroughly in the usual way to collect up any remaining debris.

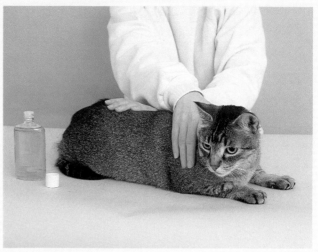

4 Use a bristle or baby brush briskly at this point. This will remove any remaining loose fur without disturbing the work already done and causing more hair to shed.

5 Now sprinkle a little bay rum lotion on the hands and, working down the cat from neck to base of tail, gently massage it into the cat's coat. This is effective on any dark-furred, tabby or dark tortie cats as it brings out the brilliance of the colours and leaves a beautiful sheen on the coat. It should not be used on light-coloured cats, as it can cause staining.

6 Finally, for a really superb finish, treat your cat to a polish with a chamois leather or a piece of silk. Always smooth the fur in the direction that it naturally lies.

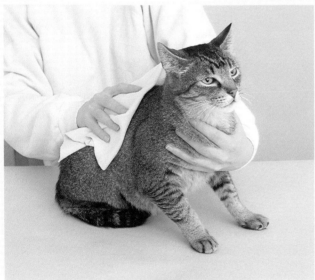

7 A well-groomed cat will look sleek, with a glossy sheen to the coat.

STEP-BY-STEP TO GROOMING A LONGHAIR CAT

Longhaired cats require regular grooming if their coats are to remain free-flowing and tangle-free. Particular attention should be paid to the underparts, especially the belly and trousers, as these are where mats and knots are most likely to occur. Matting is a little like rust on a car — once started, it tends to spread like wildfire. Regular grooming for at least fifteen minutes each evening will prevent them forming; the alternative is a regular trip to the vet for anaesthetics to be administered and the matted areas surgically removed which is unpleasant for the cat and expensive.

1 For a longhair cat you will need: (from left to right) wide-toothed comb, toothbrush, wire and bristle double-sided brush, talcum powder, metal comb with long and short teeth, slicker brush.

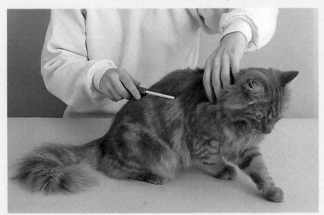

2 Use a wide-toothed comb, or even better one with alternate long and short teeth, to comb gently through the coat in the opposite direction to that in which it usually lies. It may be necessary actually to make partings in the coat and comb it in sections. It is important to make sure that you comb right through to the undercoat to free any knots and tangles, and to comb *gently* through the underparts (this is a delicate part of a cat's anatomy).

3 Lightly sprinkle the coat with baby, or any unperfumed, talcum powder; this helps to ease the brush through the fur, separating each individual hair and adding bulk to the coat. Avoid heavily perfumed 'designer' talcs which can cause an allergic reaction, particularly to the eyes.

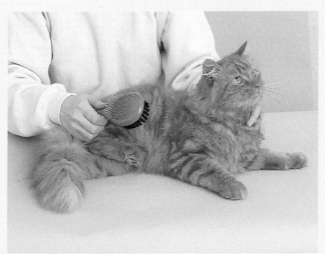

4 Brush the coat well, carefully using the wire side of the brush. Be gentle as, although the wire brush is effective, it can cause the delicate hair to break off if used too firmly. If in doubt, omit the wire brushing until you are confident of the way to do it.

5 Now use the bristle side of the brush.

6 Use a toothbrush to brush the facial area. (Most brushes are far too large for this delicate area, but an ordinary toothbrush fits the bill nicely.)

7 A 'slicker' brush, although not essential, can be used for the final stage. This is mainly for the tail and back and will give that finishing touch by fluffing up the fur.

8 The finished result; smooth and tangle-free.

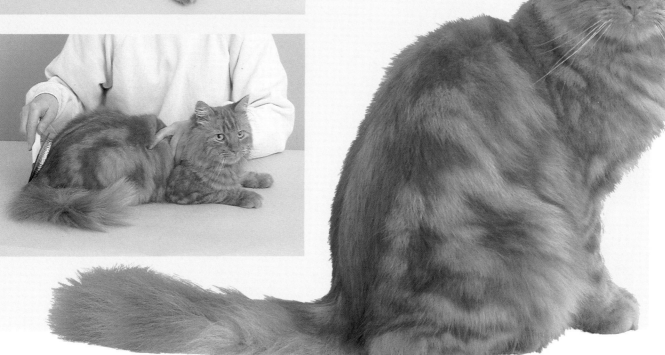

CARING FOR AN ELDERLY CAT

It is impossible to define 'elderly' in terms of years. Cats, like humans, can grow old at any age – some could be classified as elderly at eight years of age, while some still behave like kittens well into their teens. Cats, of course, do not show their age as humans do because they have furry faces, and you cannot see the lines and wrinkles.

Routine maintenance is probably the best way to prevent your cat from becoming prematurely elderly, and this should have begun from kittenhood. However, as a cat grows older, so do all its internal organs; they have served the cat for many years and are bound to start degenerating at some point. Some cats will suffer from heart problems, liver or kidney failure; others may become prone to arthritis and rheumatic problems. Some live to a ripe old age without suffering from any of these. If the cat has been well cared for all its life, then you have done all you can to minimize the chance of your cat becoming frail in old age. Remember also, that some weaknesses can be inherited and there is little you can do about that.

In general, treat your senior cat with the sort of care and respect you would a favourite grandmother. Plenty of love and attention is a priority and can work wonders; regular, balanced meals that are neither too rich nor too bland and contain a good balance of roughage will ensure that the cat is getting the essential nutrients and enough fibre for the bowels to work well; a controlled, warm environment will help to fend off chills and chest complaints; exercise will help to keep the joints mobile and the muscles toned – playing the occasional game will probably be greatly appreciated.

Watch your cat for any change in behaviour which could indicate that some vital organ is not functioning correctly; if

the problem is diagnosed before degeneration has gone too far, it will be possible to keep your cat alive for a considerable time with the correct medication. The diagnosis must be carried out by your veterinary surgeon, who will probably take a series of blood, urine and stool samples to isolate the problem. Your job is to observe and let the vet know how exactly the cat is behaving differently.

Look out for the following indications of ill health:

An apparent lack of appetite may be caused by pain from dental problems, a common complaint among older cats. Your vet will be able to examine the

ABOVE
Elderly cats often suffer from dental problems such as gum disease and loose teeth. Teeth may have to be extracted, but this will not prevent your cat from eating the foods it is used to.

RIGHT

As cats get older, they will often spend longer parts of the day asleep, but they still need to exercise to keep joints mobile and muscles toned.

mouth and tell you what, if anything, needs to be done about it.

● An increase in thirst could be indicative of diabetes or it could be caused by liver or kidney problems.

● Keep an eye, too, on the litter tray to make sure that the motions look healthy; if they appear too runny or too hard there could be a coeliac or intestinal problem.

● Incontinence could have a mechanical cause, such as paralysis of the bladder, but could just as easily be cystitis, which will often respond well to treatment.

● Watch for any lumps and bumps developing – they may be harmless, but monitor them for any change in shape that might indicate a tumour.

● EUTHANASIA ●

We all know that the end has to come sometime, however sad an occasion this may be. With our pets, we have the choice to save them suffering and humanely have them put to sleep.

Cats seem to have a high pain threshold, and will purr even when in great discomfort. When you have lived with your cat for many years, you will know it as well as an old friend; no matter

what pretence it puts on, you instinctively understand that all is not well and that it is unhappy. Cats hate being dirty; if a cat becomes incurably incontinent it must be feeling a miserable creature indeed. Some tumours are inoperable in advanced years, and a cat with cancer must surely suffer, whatever brave face it shows.

If you know your cat well, you will know when the time is coming – you have the ability to authorize your vet to curtail its suffering. Cats do not hold religious convictions so, when we have the opportunity to let them go in a peaceful and dignified manner, should we not do so?

ABOVE

A small memorial plaque in the garden will ensure that a much-loved pet is never forgotten.

WORKING CATS

Man has always had a need to domesticate animals, and for good reason. Cattle and sheep provide food, dogs are used for hunting and guarding, and cats – they are probably the most efficiently designed mousetrap ever invented! Although, today, we think of cats as domestic pets, it was not so long ago that many cats had to work for their living and some still do.

Historically, cats were used to guard the grain stores where rats and mice would be in abundance; later, in industrialized locations, they were commonly placed in factories and warehouses to control the vermin population. Mice can be very destructive, and will even chew their way through paper and cardboard. When the postal service was introduced cats were often found in sorting offices to safeguard the mail; even to this day there is a cat, retained by tradition, on the payroll of the Royal Mail at the main Mount Pleasant Sorting Office in London, although it is doubtful if he has to earn his keep! Cats are also to be seen in many different situations, including train stations, hospital grounds and traditionally in many theatres.

But it is not just through their mousing abilities that cats have helped humans, and it is possible that cats were employed as 'turnspits', as were dogs, in medieval times. In 1889 Harrison Weir,

LEFT AND BELOW
This cat lives in a garden centre; although his favourite occupation seems to be sitting on the sun-warmed stone garden ornaments, he also provides a service by warning birds away from young plants and seedlings.

the founder of the National Cat Club in the UK, wrote of many working cats: in London's Fleet Prison a resident cat caught mice and brought them to the starving prisoners; in 1828, a cat living in the British port of Plymouth was reported to have caught fish and brought the catch to hungry soldiers. He also makes reference to a missionary visiting China who reported that the cat was regarded as a time-keeper; at midday the pupils of a cat's eyes would narrow to a slit as thin as a hair, but after this time would dilate and become more rounded. This, purportedly, was one Chinese method of telling the time.

The descendants of many of these working felines can still be seen in feral cat colonies – the unwanted population of cats abandoned when their usefulness to man waned.

ABOVE
Cats can sometimes be seen in restaurants, although they should obviously be kept well away from cooking and food preparing areas.

RIGHT
Cats have traditionally been kept as mousers in warehouses and factories to control the vermin population. This cat enjoys the enviable post (probably rarely exercised) of mouser on a pet-food wholesaler's premises.

ABOVE
An office cat enjoys a snooze at the end of the day. Although unlikely to have to catch mice for a living, office cats are soothing companions in the workplace as well as at home. However, someone must always be available to look after the cat at home during holidays.

SAFEKEEPING
OF CATS

In today's environment there are many dangers lying in wait for the unsuspecting feline. Outside the home are cars and unguarded areas of water that could curtail at least one of a cat's nine lives. Even indoors there are dangers, not just from household appliances, but from toxic substances we use everyday, such as disinfectants and decorators' paint. Be aware of these risks and ensure your cat enjoys a long and happy life.

There are many dangers that a cat can encounter during its life. Most people consider that cats are only at risk if exposed to the great, wide world lurking outside the front door. This is simply not true: there are dangers within the home, too. Many cats allowed a free-ranging lifestyle gain a certain amount of 'street sense' and learn to look after themselves, within reason. Those living within the confines of the house rely totally on humans for their safety and wellbeing.

The decision to confine your cat to the home may be dictated by where you live. In modern towns and cities, many people live in apartment blocks where it is not always possible to let puss out for an evening constitutional. You may prefer to sleep sound in the knowledge that your cat is safe indoors. On the other hand, many people do not like the idea of fussing with indoor litter trays, and would not want a cat unless it used the garden for toilet purposes. (Consider the neighbours though – not everyone likes their flowerbeds used as cat toilets.)

Perhaps the best way to decide which way your cat will live, and the restrictions to impose upon it, is to look first at all the inherent dangers that it could meet with.

BELOW
Broken, brittle roofing panels and damaged wire mesh can constitute a real danger to any cat; these materials could pierce the skin and cause an infection to set in.

• OUTDOOR DANGERS •

DISEASES AND PARASITIC INFECTIONS are generally transmissible from one cat to another, so any free-ranging cat will be more prone to disease than one confined indoors. That said, these cats will acquire a certain immunity to many diseases as they are frequently exposed to low-level infections. (*See 'Health Care, Parasites, and Ailments and Illnesses' for more information.*)

FENCING AND BOUNDARIES can provide a safe area for cats as long as they are constructed in a sensible material, with no sharp barbs or other hazards. However, some people build fences to keep other people's cats out and these can be quite dangerous – electric fences and barbed wire can cause horrific damage to a domestic pet.

DOMESTIC REFUSE, left out in bins and sacks in the garden, is of great interest to any cat, not just the marauding feral. For some reason, cats seem to be especially attracted to the neighbours' leftovers. But

ABOVE
A well-fenced-in garden will allow your cat a little freedom without the risk of dangers from the outside world.

Cats love exploring, especially in territories that are otherwise forbidden to them. This cat has managed to get itself shut in the garden shed and might have remained undiscovered for some time if the owner had not made a habit of checking the shed and other outbuildings every night.

ABOVE
Cats are born scavengers and a dislodged dustbin lid is an open invitation. Most food disposed of in this way is contaminated and, if eaten, will give your cat a stomach upset at the very least.

what goes in those bins, and what damage could it cause? Leftover food decomposes quickly, especially when the weather is warm, and if eaten could cause a severe stomach upset. Some bones, particularly from cooked chicken and rabbit, are brittle and could lodge in a cat's throat with fatal consequences. Broken glass, if not properly wrapped, can cause untold damage both externally, if trodden on and, more seriously, if swallowed. Chemicals, such as washing powder, can spill over and cause toxic problems if eaten along with waste food.

OTHER CATS. If your cat is allowed free-ranging access it will inevitably meet other cats. Most will be friendly, but an un-neutered male can be a different beast. It is not unknown for such a cat to attack a kitten.

OUTBUILDINGS may not seem danger-ous, but they are if a cat gets locked in without food and water. The time of year that poses the greatest risk is autumn, when keen gardeners do a final sweep up

of leaves, and then lock all tools away for the winter in their garden shed. This is a time for great vigilance; a cat missing at this time of year is quite often to be found locked up in a neighbour's shed. Also, look at the dangers found within a garden shed: this is usually where chemicals, paint and tools are stored, all of which are potentially dangerous to a cat, so make sure that the shed door is locked when you leave, and that no cat is inside. Make sure that outbuildings and sheds are well-maintained too – broken windows and roofing tiles are potentially hazardous.

PESTICIDES AND GARDEN SPRAYS are chemicals that many keen gardeners use, but please be careful. Anything that carries a label stating 'keep away from babies and small children' should also read 'dangerous to cats', but rarely does. Slug pellets are almost lethal to a cat. Instead,

ABOVE

Garden sheds are often used to store paint, thinners, turpentine, weedkillers and other toxic chemicals. Please make sure you keep the door firmly closed as an inquisitive cat will try to gain access, often to its own detriment.

● CAT-PROOFING YOUR GARDEN ●

This may sound a daunting and expensive task, but need not be if your garden is reasonably small. Chicken wire or other wire mesh will do the job nicely, especially if your fences or surrounding walls are high in the first place. Using 47 mm by 50 mm (2 in by 2 in) upright batons, and the same for horizontal support across the top of the

fence, loosely attach the wire mesh so that the cat cannot get a firm grip and will be unable to jump into the neighbour's garden.

If your fence is weak or there are gaps at ground level, cover these areas right down to the ground and, if possible, bury the wire down to a level of about 150 mm (6 in).

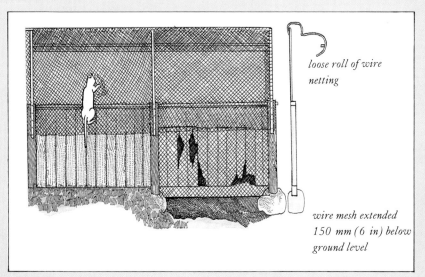

loose roll of wire netting

wire mesh extended 150 mm (6 in) below ground level

This cat is enjoying all the benefits of a sunny garden that is beautifully maintained and weed-free; the owner is sensible and uses only environmentally friendly, cat-safe pesticides.

try using a 'slug pub' (a small container sunk in the ground and filled with beer – the slugs and snails are attracted to it and drown). For greenfly and aphids, avoid chemicals that can harm cats; diluted washing-up liquid is just as effective in killing these garden pests. Look carefully on the label of any lawn fertilizer; many contain a moss killer, and this is yet another danger. Hormone weedkillers, which encourage the plants to outgrow themselves, are the safest for animals.

ROADS AND CARS. More cats die following road accidents than from any other causes. But look on the bright side – most cats do learn from their mistakes, and few get hit by a car twice. If your cat is going to be allowed to roam free, try to give it a little advance information: in a safe container, such as a cat basket, place the cat under your car. Start the engine and rev hard (for a few seconds only, or the cat will inhale too many fumes). This should persuade the cat that a car is a

BELOW
A cat allowed freedom to roam the streets is at risk both from thieves and from the possibility of a road accident.

nasty animal and, hopefully, it will remember to stay well away from traffic. It is almost a case of being cruel to be kind, but it does work.

THEFT. Cats are stolen for various reasons, the main ones being vivisection and the European fur trade. A recent problem has been the increasing popularity of fighting dogs, such as pit bull terriers, and the associated rise in theft of cats used to bait the dogs before a fight. Theft poses little threat to the cat confined at home, but those allowed to wander are at risk. Try to allow your cat freedom only when you are around in the garden to supervise. Always make sure that the cat is safely back indoors before you leave the house. *Never* put your cat out at night – this is an open invitation to any would-be thief, as it is much easier to steal anything under cover of darkness. Any cat allowed outside should wear a collar with the owner's name, address and telephone number on it. Never put the cat's

ABOVE
Cats tend to wander around parked cars. This may seem safe but if the car was moving this photograph may have told a very different story.

WHAT TO DO IF YOUR CAT GOES MISSING

Search your house thoroughly to make sure that the cat really is missing. It can be embarrassing to patrol the local area, telling all the neighbours that you have lost a cat, only to find the wiley creature asleep in the airing cupboard. Make sure that the cat is not accidentally shut in the bathroom, or is curled up in the linings of the curtains – another favourite hiding place.

Check that the cat has not got into the neighbours' house: ask them to look particularly in warm spots, such as the bedroom, boiler room and airing cupboard. Also, ask them to check outbuildings as a frightened, lost cat will seek refuge in any dark corner.

Put up notices locally, with a picture if possible, describing the cat and saying when and where it went missing. Never state anything along the lines of 'Valuable Pedigree Cat Lost', as this may encourage otherwise honest folk to keep your pet. Simply describe the way the cat looks and offer a reward for its safe return.

Tell people who are up early such as the postman, milkman and paper boy. Cats revert quickly to feral habits and tend to hide in daylight, only coming out under cover of darkness to forage for food, so early risers are more likely to spot them.

If you live near a school, ask the headteacher to make an announcement. Most children are fond of pets, and will take a little extra time on their way to and from school to look out for a missing cat.

Inform your local cat club, the breed club if your cat is a pedigree, local animal rescue centres, and the local veterinary practices.

Put an advertisement in the 'Lost and Found' section of the local paper.

Tell the police, stressing that you suspect theft of your pet. If your cat is a pedigree, this is the time to stress that it is valuable.

If all else fails, try telephoning the local street cleansing department – it is better to know the ultimate fate of your cat, and it is the road cleaners who find many of the pets that have been killed on the streets.

Never give up hope. Cats have been known to return home on their own accord after many months. Most cat clubs and rescue organizations link up with each other nationwide, and many missing cats eventually meet up again with their owners.

RIGHT

Any cat allowed outside must wear a collar and tag marked with the owner's name, address and telephone number; never *put the cat's name on the tag as this might encourage a would-be thief to entice a trusting feline away.*

name on as a trusting feline is more likely to go to a stranger when its name is called – and that stranger could be a cat thief.

TRAPS are rare in towns, but do pose a threat to cats in the countryside. Many traps are now illegal, but this does not prevent poachers from using them. Wherever possible, try to keep your cat in the garden, and regularly check surrounding woodlands – a prime target for trappers – for signs of traps, then inform the police who will safely remove any you find. Do not try to remove them yourself as they are very dangerous.

TREES. It is not a joke that cats get stuck in trees and the fire brigade has to be called. This is most likely to happen with kittens, so care should be shown when a young cat explores the garden; but adults can get stuck too in rescue attempts, and there is a limit to the number of times the fire brigade will come out when they have more important things to attend to. There is a simple tip to prevent cats getting caught up awkward trees: about

six feet from the ground, nail some chicken wire or similar (not barbed wire) on to the tree in a fan shape – the cat will not be able to get a firm grip to climb further, but will have enough tree to play and strop claws on.

WATER. Swimming pools, ponds, lakes and rivers are all potentially dangerous. To dispel a popular myth that cats hate water, most cats can swim, but not well and so water does constitute a danger. There are really only two options: either keep the cat away from water, or keep the water away from the cat. Cover swimming pools and ponds with cat-proof material, such as chicken wire. Large lakes, rivers and streams are more difficult to make safe; again, chicken wire can be used to fence them off. Alternatively, if this is not practicable, keep cats indoors or confined to a suitable outside run.

● CAT RUNS ●

A cat run may be another option, especially if your garden is huge, and they need not look too unsightly. Many breeders of pedigree cats have purpose-built cat houses and runs constructed in their gardens, which do look somewhat obvious. However, a small area annexed off near the house with direct access from the main building, such as through a window or door from the kitchen or back room, will allow your cat to potter in and out without any risk of theft. Make sure that it is sturdily built, using heavier wood than that suggested for cat-proofing a garden, covered in wire mesh and roofed – this is important, as otherwise the cat could climb up the wire and disappear into the world beyond. To maximize the light, use acrylic sheets, such as Perspex or Plexiglass for the roof and, again, climbing plants can be grown around the wire mesh to make the end result more pleasing to the eye. Some cat runs can look almost like little conservatories without walls.

A small cat run built adjacent to the house will provide your cat with both safety and access to fresh air.

*There are possibly more dangers to be found in the kitchen than in any other single room in the house. After use the owner has thoughtfully placed an empty saucepan over the ceramic hot plate (**RIGHT**); this however has warmed and so the kitten has decided to curl up in the pan. A potentially more dangerous situation (**BELOW**), the cat investigates a pan containing boiling fish.*

• INDOOR DANGERS •

Inside a nice warm house you might think that a cat is relatively safe, but is it? Take a look round your house room by room. Consider the dangers, and the associated safety precautions that you would extend to a human toddler, and apply the same for your cat.

KITCHENS are usually the focal point of a household. Any sensible cat will want to take part in the everyday hubbub of meals being cooked, people chatting, machines whirring and above all, the warmth that exudes from this hotbed of domesticity — all cats like to feel part of the family.

Never leave pots and pans unattended. Interesting cooking smells will attract your cat, inviting it to investigate further. The result could be: at worst, a severe scald or burn; at best, your supper simply disappearing.

Hob plates, especially the ceramic variety, remain hot for some time after use. Never let a cat near these unless there is a covering lid that can be pulled over the entire hob. Failing this, place a saucepan full of cold water over the hot hob to absorb most of the heat, or keep the cat out of the kitchen until the appliance has cooled down.

Washing machines and tumble driers have some sort of fatal attraction for cats. Have you noticed how cats like to watch

RIGHT
Although a grown-up cat such as this is unlikely to drown in a bowl of soapy water, for a small kitten this would be a definite risk.

Cats are fascinated by electrical appliances and will frequently try to chew through the cables, much to the annoyance of their owners. Moreover, if a cat managed to sever a mains lead it would suffer a life-threatening electric shock.

get food poisoning from dirty work surfaces. But what disinfectant do you use? Cats like to walk around the kitchen, and are probably fed in this room too, so it is hard to keep them off the work surfaces. Cats can absorb all sorts of poisons and toxins through their paw pads, and some disinfectants contain phenols and cresols which can be lethal to cats. Check the label on your disinfectant carefully. Some products do not state all their constituents; avoid these and choose one you know to be safe.

BATHROOMS. The main danger here is water, and the possibility of drowning. If you fill the bath, never leave it unattended or, if you do, make sure the bathroom door is closed so cats cannot get in. The same applies to the hand basin. A cat can be scalded badly in a hot bath so always run the cold water tap first or, if you have mixers, make sure the temperature is correct; cats move quickly and can dive for the bath before you have time to

BELOW

Cats love to sit in the kitchen and carry out their ablutions; having walked over the work surface the cat is now washing its paws. Most owners know which disinfectants are cat-friendly; be sure that the brand you buy contains no phenols or cresols.

the washing going round in the machine? (Mine find the spin programme particularly interesting.) But washers can be fatal to cats. Never leave the door open, as a cat will quite happily jump in and go to sleep if the appliance is still warm. It is then so easy to throw in the laundry and switch on the machine, resulting in one very clean but very dead cat. The same applies to tumble driers which can suffocate a cat trapped inside. Make a simple house rule: never close the door and switch on the machines until a head count has been made of resident felines. Put a sticker on the door of the machines to this effect so that even visitors know the rules.

Sinks full of water can cause drowning. Although an adult cat is unlikely to drown in a kitchen sink, a small kitten could easily do so. When your sink is not in use, pull the plug or empty the bowl.

Disinfectants are part of everyday life and so they should be, especially where food is being prepared. No one wants to

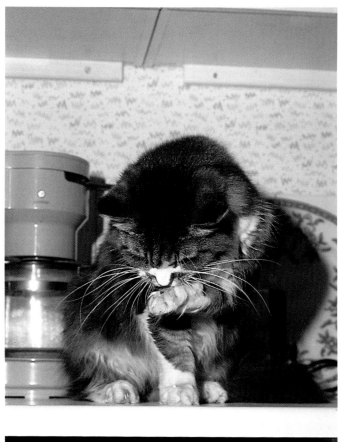

RIGHT
An open fire should always be encased with a fire guard.

LEFT
For some reason cats seem to like dirty laundry and will even sleep in the laundry basket; check your laundry thoroughly before putting it in the washing machine just in case there is a cat lurking in the depths.

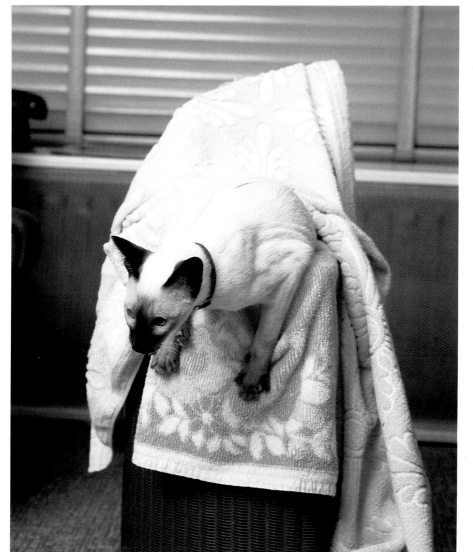

ABOVE
*Some houseplants can
also present a hazard
for cats; poinsettia and
mistletoe, to name just
two plants often found
in the home, are both
poisonous. Check plant
guides to verify that
the plants you have in
the home and garden
are safe.*

● POISONOUS PLANTS ●

*There are many plants that are
dangerous to cats. Some, such as
laburnum seeds, are fatal if eaten, but
many others can cause serious stomach
upsets. Even houseplants and cut
flowers can create problems. Most cats
know instinctively when a plant is
poisonous and will avoid it. If in
doubt, contact your vet who should be
able to advise you. Some cats develop
allergies, in much the same way as
some humans are prone to hay fever,
and suffer a reaction to certain plants
and trees.*

A pretty picture this may seem, but
remember that there may be many plants
in your garden which are poisonous to
cats.

close the door. There is also a danger with the toilet; many people use chemical blocks, that clean with every flush. Most of these are highly toxic, so always keep the toilet lid down if your cat has access to this room.

OTHER DANGERS lurk in every room that contains electric power points and their associated appliances. Cats, being naturally inquisitive and playful, believe that electric cables, wires and telephone leads have all been devised as cat toys, and love to chew through them. Some years ago a friend of mine spent Christmas Day resuscitating his cat after she chewed through the wire of the Christmas tree lights. The cat survived thanks to his swift actions, but not everybody knows how to effect mouth-to-nose resuscitation on a cat (*see 'Health Care'*). If your cat is a wire chewer, put special conduit over the lead of each appliance (shower hose works very well, but is a little unsightly): most electrical shops will help you.

Common household paraphernalia such as sewing boxes contain needles and pins, which can be fatal to a cat. Balls of wool and bobbins of cotton can get wound around a cat's tongue making it swell up, cause choking and, eventually, suffocation. Even the desk drawer can reveal dangers, such as rubber bands and paper clips which can harm a cat in much the same way as cotton and needles.

CHEMICALS of various kinds are kept in the home, the obvious ones being cleaning materials, but also DIY products such as glues and solvents, paint thinners, turpentine and even paint itself, all of which can be toxic. Any such substances should be kept well out of the way of cats – and children for that matter – preferably in a room or shed where they have no access.

When redecorating, *read all labels very carefully*. Nearly all modern paint products, wallpaper paste, size and wood preservatives contain fungicides and

other antibacterial agents. These can be lethal to cats. Keep cats out of rooms that are being decorated, until all fumes have disappeared. Also, because cats can absorb toxins through their paw pads – even from wallpaper paste splashes that end up on the floor – make sure that floors have been swabbed down after decorating.

OPEN WINDOWS. Cats that are confined to a flat or house need fresh air, but any worthwhile member of the feline species will soon realize how to get out of an open window, with dire consequences if it happens to be on the eighth floor. It is simple to make a wooden frame, covered with wire mesh that will fit snugly over a window frame, allowing fresh air to circulate and your cat to be safe.

BALCONIES are another problem – nice to sit out on during warm summer evenings, but your cat will want to join you and could jump over the side. Even more possible is that the cat will try to jump to any overhanging tree nearby. Again, chicken wire on a wooden frame works quite well as a deterrent – and you have the added bonus that the wire can be covered with climbing plants.

ABOVE
Some cats confined to an apartment are lucky enough to have access to a balcony or roof garden. As these are usually several storeys up it is advisable to safeguard your cat from falling by placing trellis or wire mesh around this area – if unsightly, it can be concealed with climbing plants.

BREEDING
FROM YOUR CAT

*Cat breeding is a delightful, but expensive, hobby.
Few breeders actually make money from selling kittens and,
for the vast majority, cat breeding is a pleasurable pastime
and a very good way of making new, like-minded friends.
Here you will find all the necessary information on mating,
kittening and caring for the mother cat and her kittens.*

The decision to breed from your cat should be made only after careful consideration. If you have bought a pedigree cat, it will have cost you a considerable amount of money. You may have seen that the queen produced six or seven kittens, or even more, and it does not take a mathematical genius to work out that the proceeds from the sale of those kittens seem to amount to a hefty credit to the breeder's bank balance. This may tempt you to breed from your pedigree cat – although in the UK it will probably have been placed on the non-active register as many breeders discourage novices from breeding; the equivalent in the USA would be 'not for breeding' noted on the blue slip.

Or, maybe you have acquired a pretty non-pedigree cat and feel that it should be allowed to have at least one litter of kittens before being spayed.

Please think again about your reasons for wanting to breed from your cat, and consider whether you are able to afford kittens that, through your choice, have been brought into the world. Whether the cat has a pedigree as long as your arm, or is the result of an accidental mating, the resulting kittens are still living beings that will rely on you completely for a good start in life; they are *your* responsibility. Pedigree or not, they will cost you the same amount to raise, and should be given the same respect when it comes to finding suitable homes.

If you consider cat breeding a profitable business that can bring you added income with the minimum of time and effort, you are in for a shock.

BELOW
A sensible breeder will regularly weigh the kittens to ensure that they are progressing well; this mother cat obviously has other ideas.

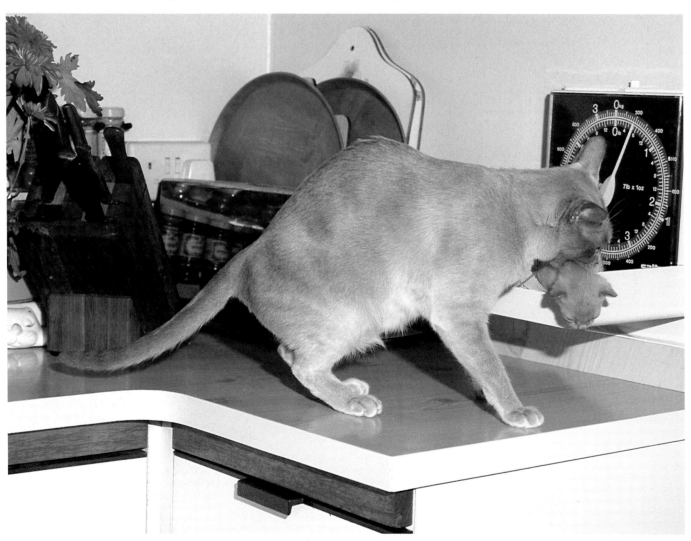

Most usually it is the mother cat that will attend to all her kittens' needs. This family group is unusual in as much as the father is helping out too.

RIGHT
These three young Seal-point Siamese kittens clearly show the colour markings on face, ears, legs and tail expected of the breed in maturity.

RIGHT

The operation to spay a female cat is relatively quick and she will usually only need twenty-four hours to recuperate. The resulting small scar and bald patch on the flank will be only temporary.

ABOVE
Cats do make wonderful mothers, but unless there is a specific breeding programme in mind it is kinder to have the cat neutered and not add to the ever-increasing kitten population.

Consider the expenses involved:
- Stud fee
- Testing for FeLV and other transmissible diseases
- Heating for the kittens
- Special diet for the mother cat during pregnancy and lactation
- Feeding of kittens after weaning
- Vitamin and mineral supplements
- Advertising the kittens for sale
- Stationery needed for pedigrees, and diet sheets
- Inoculations
- Registration and transfer fees

There is also the chance that there may be a hiccup in the pregnancy, kittening or weaning period, any of which will involve veterinary expenses. It is not unknown for a novice breeder to lose several kittens in the litter unless there is someone experienced available to give advice; it is possible that only one or two kittens in the first litter will survive to twelve weeks of age. This cuts down the profit margin considerably, and the breeder needs to be able to absorb these costs.

No matter how thoroughly you have checked out a prospective owner of one of your feline offspring, there is the chance that it will be returned to you. Marriages fail, houses are repossessed, a new baby

may come along: all of these can be reasons for a cat needing to be rehomed, and it is up to you as the breeder to assume the responsibility. Do you have the facilities to take the cat or kitten back, or will it become just another rescue statistic? And, are you knowledgeable enough to advise a prospective owner about cat health and welfare?

So, breeding cats is an expensive and demanding hobby but, given dedication to the mother cat and her offspring, it will give you many hours of pleasure. A mother cat playing with her kittens will provide far more entertainment than anything you could find to watch on the television.

TO NEUTER OR NOT TO NEUTER

For any cat destined to become a family pet, the kindest thing to do is to neuter it. An un-neutered tom will become a nuisance not just in your own home, but also to the neighbours if it is allowed a free-ranging life. A calling

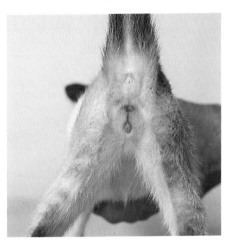

*If you are in any doubt as to the sex of your cat or kitten, consult these photographs: male (**LEFT**) and female (**BELOW**).*

queen will be just as, if not more, noisy than a male; comparable with a baby crying continuously, only louder.

Unless you have a specific breeding programme in mind, or have definite homes for all the possible kittens, neutering is the most sensible and responsible course of action.

Neutering ('altering', in the USA) is a simple operation. In the male it takes little time; an incision is made in the scrotum, each testis pulled out separately, the vas deferens severed, the testis removed, and a suture inserted. For a female, it involves abdominal surgery, but still does not take long. Usually, an incision is made about 1 cm (½ in) long on the cat's flank; in an older cat this may be done mid-line, with a longer incision straight up the underside of the belly. The ovaries and uterus are removed, and the opening stitched up. Many veterinary surgeons use dissolvable sutures, so there is no need to return to the surgery. In general, it takes only about two minutes to castrate a male, and five minutes to spay a female, so they are subjected to a minimum of anaesthetic and recover very quickly; a male will often be up and bouncing when you bring it back home, though a female may require twenty-four hours to convalesce.

It is best not to neuter your cat at too young an age; about six months is right. Neutering before this, when the endocrine system is not fully developed can cause hormonal problems, such as miliary eczema, in later life. If your kitten is female, and calls precociously, she can be given contraception, either by weekly pill or injection, until she is of a suitable size and age to undergo her operation. Male cats can be similarly precocious, and may try to mate, spray or both; if this is the case, it is better not to delay neutering.

One word of warning; cats are not hampered by morals and it is not unknown for siblings to mate each other; if you buy a pair of kittens at the same time,

watch out for signs of the female calling, or you may end up becoming a cat breeder before you would like to.

If you have decided to breed from your cat, and are sure that you will be able to find good homes for all the kittens, you must decide on a suitable stud cat.

FINDING A SUITABLE STUD CAT

The first place to start this search is with the breeder of your own cat, who will probably be able to recommend a genetically compatible sire. It is inadvisable to mate together cats that are closely related, such as mother to son or father to daughter, unless you are an experienced breeder; even then, it should really only be done to double-check that your line is not carrying deformities. Alternatively, contact the breed club who

ABOVE
Stud cats are usually housed in their own special stud quarters as most of them spray and can be somewhat anti-social within a domestic home.

should be able to give you an independent opinion of a reputable stud owner.

If possible, try not to take your maiden queen too far away for her first mating. Calling will be a new experience to her and she will be feeling a little confused; putting her in a cat carrier and driving her many miles from home will make her more upset and might cause her to come 'off call'.

When you think that you have found a suitable stud cat, go and visit the premises. Your queen will be staying there for several days, if not a week, and it is best to be sure you are happy with the stud cat, his owner, and the care, attention and accommodation offered to your female. If you are in any doubt, go elsewhere. Do not be swayed by impressive rosettes advertising the stud cat's wins; it is not always the Grand Champion that sires the best and healthiest kittens, nor his owner who will give your cat the best attention during her stay. Do not be impressed by the stud owner who has many studs available, either; stud cats are usually

housed in outside runs and, if there are several such cats available, can you be sure that they are all receiving the care that they need and, more importantly, that your cat will receive the same?

If all seems in order and you wish to proceed with the mating, the stud owner will ask you many questions.

Documents the stud owner will ask to see are:
- Pedigree certificate
- Registration document
- Inoculation certificate
- FeLV/FIV negative certificates
- Pet name of cat
- Favourite diet

A stud owner needs to know the exact parentage of a cat she or he accepts into stud; that the cat is registered in the owner's name, and that the breeder has registered it to allow for breeding. The inoculation and FeLV/FIV neg certificates assure the stud owner that risks of infections to her cat are kept to a minimum.

As a stud cat will spend most of its life confined to quarters the responsible owner will ensure that these are as luxurious as possible.

This works both ways, and the stud owner will show you her cat's certificates too. Your cat's preferred diet and use of its pet name will also make it settle in that much more quickly.

WHEN IS YOUR CAT READY TO BE MATED?

Cats can be precocious creatures, some breeds more than others. It is not unknown for a sixteen-week-old kitten to start calling. This is far too young to contemplate a formal mating; wait until she is at least a year old.

A female cat is called a queen for good reason, which has nothing to do with royalty. It comes from the old word quean, meaning a whore or a hussy. When you hear your cat call, and see her pedalling her back legs and exposing her rear end, this makes sense! When your queen first comes on call, contact the stud owner and tell her. It is best to mate your cat on the second or third day of call, but an experienced stud owner may advise you to bring a novice queen to her stud as soon as possible.

The stud owner should monitor any matings and, when sure that the cats have successfully mated, ring to ask you to take the queen away. At this point, you should be given a mating certificate with all the details of the stud cat's pedigree, the dates of mating and the date on which the kittens should be born.

CARE OF YOUR CAT DURING PREGNANCY

About twenty-one days after your cat has been mated you should be able to tell if it has been successful; at this point the nipples should be slightly swollen and show a deep pink hue. If so, you have a pregnant cat on your hands and should change her diet accordingly. If you are in any doubt, your vet should be able to confirm your opinion, or contact the stud owner who will be used to dealing with pregnant cats.

As soon as you are certain that your cat is pregnant it is advisable to introduce vitamin supplements in her food; she will undoubtedly have more than one growing kitten inside her and will need all the help she can get. Calcium can be beneficial as it helps to promote the development of strong bones in the kittens. Your vet should be able to suggest various compound powders that will supply all the other additional vitamins and minerals, if

*The stud cat, when mating a queen, will find added grip if a mat is provided for him. The stud cat grasps the queen by the scruff of her neck (**LEFT**), and positions the queen squarely ready for penetration (**BELOW**).*

LEFT
The pregnant queen will be visibly plumper and the nipples most apparent.

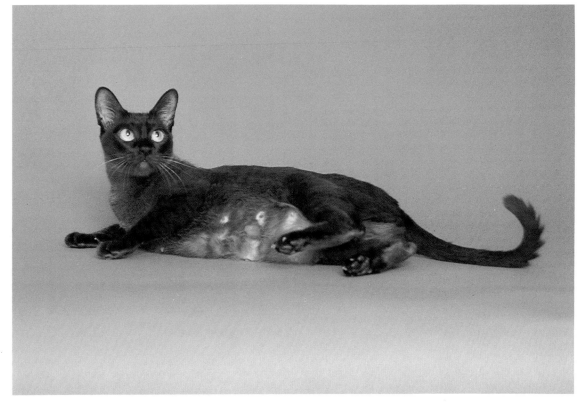

RIGHT
This very obviously pregnant cat is only a day or two away from kittening.

this is necessary, and will also tell you how long to continue giving these supplements. Many experienced breeders have found that their pregnant cats also benefit from raspberry leaf, which should be given from the fifth week of pregnancy until at least a week after kittening.

The gestation period for a cat is sixty-five days, although this may vary a day or two either side. Unless the cat seems unduly upset there is no need for panic if the cat does not produce exactly on the sixty-fifth day. A few days before the event, your cat will probably start nesting. This may not be in the place most convenient for you, and could well be in your bedroom cupboard, drawer, or linen cupboard. If possible, provide your cat with a suitable nesting box; this can be as simple as a cardboard box placed somewhere that suits you in a quiet, darkened corner. A kitten pen is ideal for containing the nest; if you are planning only one litter, you may find that the breeder of your cat will lend you one. If so, make sure you disinfect it first with a cat-friendly substance.

Line the box with alternate layers of cotton fabric and newspaper; kittening can be a messy business and it is important for the kittens to be kept as warm and dry as possible. By layering the kittening box you can remove soiled bedding after the arrival of each kitten.

◦ THE BIRTH ◦

If you are a novice breeder and have any queries or doubts before or during the birthing process, contact an experienced breeder or the owner of your cat's stud for advice. Don't call the vet at this point; not all vets are cat breeders and therefore see only problematic births. However, it is likely that all will go well and according to plan. Most cats find kittening easy, and have no problem delivering their litter efficiently.

The first sign of impending birth will be 'a bubble' appearing outside the vulva

– this is the bulging bag of waters; at this point the waters will burst and the cat should be visibly contracting. Cats are designed for multiple births, unlike humans; this means they have several, small babies, not one huge one, and so in general have an easier time. Most cats will purr all through the delivery and will only rest when all the kittens are safely born. It is always as well to be prepared to act as midwife and you should be prepared to have *clean* towels (or kitchen roll), blunt-tipped scissors and a bowl of boiled water handy in case your cat needs assistance.

Cats usually know exactly what to do, but an inexperienced maiden queen can get confused; she should bite through the umbilical cord, releasing the kitten from its placenta, and wash the kitten thoroughly with her raspy tongue to stimulate the circulation. This does not always happen and you may have to cut through the umbilical cord and stimulate the kit-

ABOVE
A kitten box makes an ideal nesting area. Before the birth, line the base with alternate layers of cotton fabric and newspaper and provide soft, warm bedding once the kittens have arrived.

ten yourself. Cut about 4 cm (1½ in) from the kitten, and remember to squeeze the cord immediately below the point at which it is severed to stem the blood flow and help the end of the cord to clot and close. Then, rub the kitten vigorously.

If the kitten does not appear to be breathing, you must take immediate action. It is likely that it has water in its lungs from inhaling the amniotic fluid, and this must be expressed quickly. Take the kitten in your hand, grasping it firmly, and using your index finger as support for its head with a motion similar to an over-arm cricket throw, swing the kitten firmly (but do not let go). This

should get rid of any fluid in the lungs.

Each kitten is attached to its own placenta, which has at this point served its main purpose – to supply nutrition to the kitten while still in the womb. The placenta now has a different function, which is to supply a quick, nutritious meal for the mother cat which will stimulate the supply of milk. Although at least one placenta should be eaten, it is not necessary for her to eat them all. Some years ago a well-intentioned novice breeder rang me to say that his cat had eaten all her placentas; she had apparently given up after the second one and so the owner gently sautéed the remaining six in a little butter and garlic to make a temp-

◉ KITTENING ◉

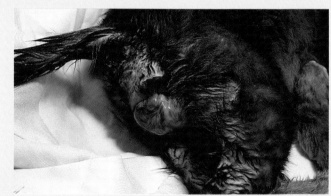

A kitten, still encased in its amniotic sac, is being delivered.

The mother chews through the umbilical cord.

The mother cat's raspy tongue not only helps to clean and dry the newborn kittens, but also acts as a stimulus to encourage circulation.

The proud mother with her family of five a couple of days after the birth.

● NO CAUSE FOR ALARM ●

Some of the processes of birth may seem a little disturbing if you have never seen them before, but they are all perfectly normal and are no cause for alarm. The general pattern of kittening involves some messy stages:

● Shortly before the birth of the first kitten a plug of mucus will come away. Even if this happens as early as a week before the kittening is due, do not worry unless the mucus has an unhealthy greenish hue or blood is discharged.

● Kittening is a stressful experience and it is not uncommon for a kitten to *suffer foetal distress; this is equally common in human babies and usually simply means that the force of delivery causes the bowels to empty and faeces to be expelled.*

● Birth is a bloody business, do not be distressed by the amount of red-tinged secretions that will be seen. The mother may continue oozing in this manner for a few days. If the colour changes, or the discharge becomes more profuse, contact the vet immediately as this could indicate a life-threatening infection to both mother and kittens.

---

ting breakfast for her. This is perhaps taking things a little too far!

It is sometimes possible for a maiden to confuse a kitten with placenta, in which case she may try to eat the kittens and suckle the afterbirth; this is why it is important to monitor your cat's kittening in case she makes a mistake.

It is helpful to make a list itemizing each kitten's time of birth and sex, and checking that each birth was accompanied by a complete placenta. This last point is important because the afterbirth may not be expelled immediately. Any afterbirth retained within the mother can cause serious infection. If in doubt, contact your vet immediately.

The whole procedure could take as little as an hour or could last half a day. Unless your cat seems ill at ease there is no cause to worry; let nature take its course. If she seems to strain, or a kitten appears stuck, it is wise to contact your vet or the stud owner, either of whom should be able to give you advice.

● AFTERCARE OF KITTENS ●

For the first few weeks the mother will supply all the kittens' needs. She will feed them, wash them and keep them warm. At about ten days or so the kittens will open their eyes and will start taking an interest in the world outside their nest. By the time they are about three weeks old they will be wanting to venture farther afield. At this age it is sensible to warn your family to watch where they step, as it is all too easy to curtail a small kitten's life with a hefty blow from a foot. (This is where a kitten pen comes into its own.) From the moment they become mobile until they are ready to leave your home when they are twelve weeks old, you must be on a constant vigil.

The kittens will become more and more inquisitive and by the time they are four or five weeks old they will be willing to lap food. The best weaning foods are those prepared for human babies, but minced chicken or fish is usually quite acceptable; pilchards are excellent as they smell strong and encourage the kittens to eat, but only give them small amounts to whet their appetites as it is a very rich food.

By the time kittens are six weeks old they should be able to eat regular cat foods. It is important that you get your kittens used to a varied diet of different brands so they do not become faddy eaters in later life.

At about ten weeks your kittens will be

Continued page 102

KITTEN DEVELOPMENT

LEFT
Kittens are born with their eyes sealed and will do little for the first few days other than suckle and sleep.

BELOW LEFT
At about ten days old the kitten's eyes will open.

BELOW RIGHT
At about three weeks old the ears will assume an upright position, making the kitten look more like a miniature version of the adult cat it will become.

RIGHT
By the time the kittens are six weeks old they should be weaned and happy to eat solid food.

BELOW RIGHT
Under strict supervision, ten-week-old kittens are ready to explore the garden for the first time.

BOTTOM
Twelve weeks old, fully inoculated and weaned, these youngsters are now ready to go to their new homes.

ready for the first of their two inoculations. This is a straightforward procedure
but the occasional kitten may suffer an
adverse vaccine reaction. This is not
serious and will probably only cause the
affected kitten to be slightly unwell for a
day or two, possibly with the odd snuffle
or sneeze. For this reason it is always
advisable to keep the kittens for three or
four days after they have been inoculated,
to allow for recovery, before letting them
go to their new homes.

ANTISOCIAL HABITS IN KITTENS

Kittens are often preoccupied with
faecal matter. This can be displayed
in one of two ways.

They may become overly interested in
their cat litter to the point where they try
to eat it. This is often because the litter
tray is too clean; always leave a little
urine-soaked litter in the tray after changing it. This should encourage the kitten
to realize what the tray has been put down
for. Or, forget the idea of using litter at
all, and substitute torn or shredded paper
until the kitten has realized the tray is for
toilet purposes. If the kitten ingests cat
litter, particularly a wood-based variety,
this will swell in the stomach and could
cause a blockage which would require
veterinary treatment.

Although it is unusual, some kittens
are 'dirty' and this is an exceedingly hard
habit to break. Once such behaviour has
been initiated by one kitten it is not
unusual for the whole litter to follow suit.
The most common reason is that the litter
tray is not clean enough and so the kittens
feel the need to defecate elsewhere. It is
possible to buy cat repellents but you
should not use these where very young
kittens are in the house. One tip: cats and
kittens do not like eating in an area that
has been soiled, so try putting the food
bowls over the preferred spot for defeca-
tion and you should find that the problem
is overcome very quickly. If the place is

inaccessible to food bowls, try covering it
with tin foil or plastic sheeting; few cats
like the sound of their excrement falling
onto these surfaces.

SELLING YOUR KITTENS

If you already have suitable homes
lined up, invite the prospective owners to visit the kittens frequently. The
kittens will not be fully inoculated until
they are twelve weeks old and so visitors
must be subjected to strict hygiene procedures. Always get them to wash their
hands with a disinfectant solution before
handling the young kittens. Early handling by the new owners is important as
this will give them the opportunity to
form a bond with the kitten that is to
become a part of their household.

If your cat has produced more kittens
than you have homes for, you may need
to advertise. Most breed clubs offer the
service of a kitten list and this is a good
place to start — the prospective buyer has
at least gone to the bother of finding out
about the relevant breed club. You can
also advertise in local papers and specialist cat magazines. From these sources the
purchasers are an unknown entity and it
is up to you to question them thoroughly
to ensure their suitability (*see 'Where to
Find a Cat and How to Choose One'*).

LEFT
Kittens love to play and explore new areas; although the hob unit was switched off and cold, it is inadvisable to encourage kittens to play in the kitchen where many dangers lurk.

PROBLEMS DURING BREEDING

There are just a few problems that can affect either the mother cat or her kittens during the early weeks. Don't be unduly alarmed by these descriptions, but observe your charges closely so prompt action can be taken, if necessary.

*Sometimes, a mother cat is unable to supply all the milk her kittens need, especially if it is a large litter; with a family of four (**BELOW**) she is unlikely to have any problems. Occasionally, mastitis may also prevent the cat from feeding her young. Kittens can fare well if foster fed with evaporated milk diluted with water (see Lack of Milk), as this healthy youngster demonstrates (**RIGHT**).*

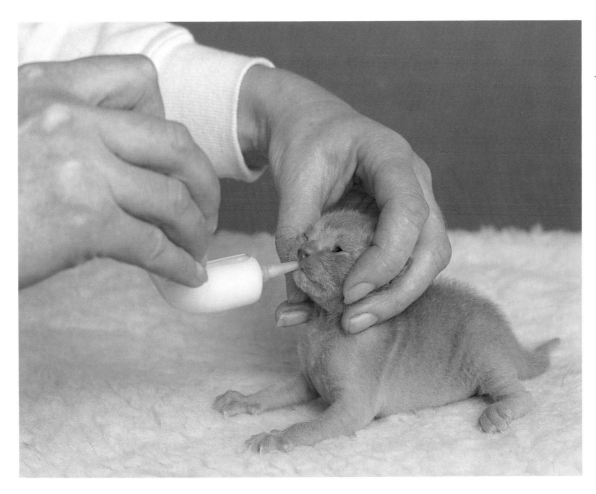

LEFT
*If for whatever reason the mother is unable to feed her kittens, this specially designed kitten foster feeder bottle will enable you to provide the kittens with the nourishment they need. (*See Lack of Milk, below.*)*

• INTUSSUSCEPTION •

DESCRIPTION

This is not common and is a bowel disorder where the intestine doubles back on itself in telescopic fashion, causing an obstruction. The symptoms are lack of appetite and no evidence of stools being passed, because the intestine is blocked.

ACTION

In a minor case it is possible to operate and remove the offending portion of bowel; in a compound case the prognosis is not good and the affected kitten will probably have to be humanely destroyed by your vet.

• LACK OF MILK •

DESCRIPTION

In general, mother's milk is generated by supply and demand; if the kittens are not hungry or indeed well enough to wish to suckle, the mother's supply of milk will dry up. Mastitis (*see right*) is another cause of this. In a very large litter the mother may not have enough milk to go round.

ACTION

If the litter is large, you will need to rotate the kittens, then top up with a foster feeder bottle containing evaporated milk diluted one part milk to three parts cooled boiled water. Proprietary cat milk substitutes are available but they can sometimes cause constipation in small kittens.

• MASTITIS •

DESCRIPTION

Mastitis usually affects the lactating queen. The symptoms are of general ill health, and the most obvious sign is that one or several of the mammary glands is impacted and feels hot and lumpy to the touch. The danger here, if the queen is still suckling, is that the kittens will drink infected milk and so suffer a form of poisoning.

ACTION

It is important to ensure that the kittens do not suckle from an infected gland; you can do this by bandaging over the affected nipple, but your vet will advise the best course of action. It is also important to get the queen to the vet as soon as possible, for a confirmed diagnosis, advice, and prescription of a suitable course of antibiotics.

• PYOMETRA •

DESCRIPTION

This can affect a cat at any age but is more likely to occur after kittening. It is an infection of the uterus and is most commonly indicated by a thick, creamy secretion from the vulva.

ACTION

In mild cases it can be treated with antibiotics but if severe, it requires the removal of the reproductive organs – that is, the cat has to be spayed.

HEALTH CARE

*Cats are generally healthy creatures but they will benefit from
annual inoculations and health-checks. Inoculations are
extremely important to safeguard cats from certain feline
diseases, but there are many illnesses and ailments from which
you cannot protect your cat in this way. Yet, by following
a routine system of care, any changes in your cat can be
immediately detected and veterinary diagnosis and treatment
sought. Accidents can happen, too, and this chapter covers all
these aspects of cat ownership, advising on symptoms,
what action to take and treatment.*

INOCULATIONS

Most cats only see the vet once a year for the booster inoculation. At this annual visit, get the vet to check the cat over thoroughly; think of it as an annual health screen. Most illnesses, if spotted at an early stage, are treatable. Immunization is now available against many feline diseases, but diseases do vary from country to country, so check with your vet which vaccines are applicable to your cat.

Some cats, like humans, feel a little unwell after inoculations; they may even suffer from a stomach upset for a day or two, but this is no cause for worry unless it persists after forty-eight hours. The important thing is to give your cat as much protection as possible against feline diseases.

Your cat should have been inoculated before it comes to your house; if not, have this done as soon as possible. If you already have cats, keep the newcomer separated from the others until this has been done. Afterwards isolate the cat for seven days; it is possible for it to 'shed' virus for several days after inoculation.

As new diseases emerge, research vets and virologists try to isolate the viruses, and provide immunization against them. In recent years there has been considerable coverage by the popular press concerning feline leukaemia virus (FeLV) and feline immuno-deficiency virus (FIV), and calling these viruses 'feline AIDS'. This is a quite incorrect description and only serves to worry people unnecessarily. Other infections, such as feline infectious peritonitis (FIP) and chlamydia, are viruses that the veterinary profession are currently working on.

Various new vaccines have been, or are being, developed against some of these viruses, but not all have been approved for commercial use in every country, so availability varies. For current information, contact your veterinary surgeon.

RIGHT

By the age of twelve weeks, the kitten should have had a full course of inoculations.

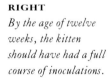

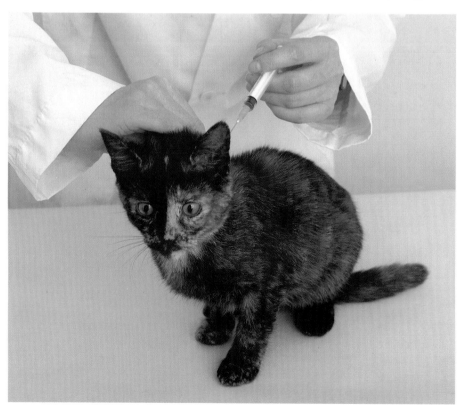

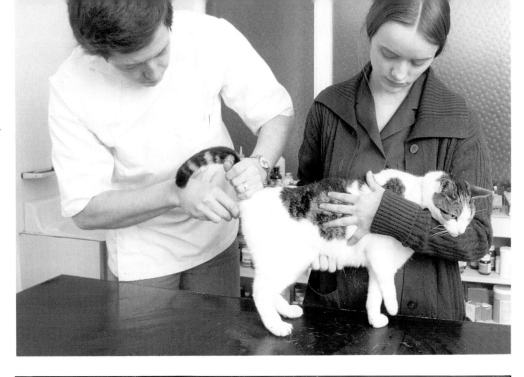

◦ FELINE INFECTIOUS ENTERITIS ◦

DESCRIPTION/SYMPTOMS

This is a virus that attacks a widespread area, but particularly the bowels and the central nervous system. The symptoms of feline infectious enteritis (FIE) are many and varied; they may not all be present. Usually, the cat will have a hunched appearance, seem generally unwell, and may appear depressed. Vomiting, diarrhoea, and then dehydration will also be apparent.

ACTION

If your cat shows any of these signs, contact the vet as soon as possible, listing the symptoms; FIE is extremely infectious between cats, but does not live long outside a feline host. For this reason, the vet may prefer to make a home visit, rather than have the cat visit the surgery. If FIE is confirmed, there is little hope for recovery.

VACCINE

This is the single most important inoculation and is usually administered at ten to twelve weeks of age, followed by an annual booster. It is possible to inoculate against FIE and cat flu with a combined vaccine.

◦ CAT FLU ◦

DESCRIPTION/SYMPTOMS

This is a general term used to describe two viruses that affect the upper respiratory tract; feline calici virus (FCV) and feline viral rhinotracheitis (FVR), a herpes virus.

FCV may only cause snuffles and sneezes, but it can also create more serious problems such as ulceration, especially of the nose, mouth and tongue. FVR affects the nose, trachea and lungs, and can cause severe respiratory problems.

With both FCV and FVR, the cat will most typically be coughing and sneezing, with a runny discharge from eyes, nose and throat, and will show a loss of appetite.

ACTION

Cat flu is likely to be most serious in a kitten or an elderly cat and, if it is not treated immediately, can result in death. In an otherwise healthy adult, the symptoms are as severe but the cat has more stamina to recover. If the cat does recover, there is always the risk that they have become a carrier of the disease and may shed virus under stress, which could infect other cats. Any known carrier should be isolated, or taken to a home where there are no other cats that could be put at risk.

VACCINE

The combined vaccine for FCV, FVR and FIE is the most commonly used today, giving maximum available protection to your cat. It is a two-stage process, with the inoculations administered three weeks apart, usually starting at between nine and twelve weeks of age, depending on the particular vaccine used. Some brands are administered as a liquid squirted into the nostrils; these are usually live vaccines, and are not suitable for all cats. Your vet will advise you on the best vaccine for your cat or kitten.

• FELINE IMMUNO-DEFICIENCY VIRUS •

DESCRIPTION/SYMPTOMS

This is a virus that attacks the immune system, and is more similar in structure to the human counterpart HIV than FELV (*see below*), but is still not transmissible between the two species. It also breaks down the immune system, but infected cats may enjoy long periods of good health before secondary infections become apparent.

ACTION

As with FELV, the presence of feline immuno-deficiency virus (FIV) can be detected in the blood. If your vet feels that the cause of illness may be related to FIV, he will organize for blood tests to be carried out.

VACCINE

Much research is being carried out, and it is hoped that an inoculation for FIV will be available soon.

• FELINE LEUKAEMIA VIRUS •

DESCRIPTION/SYMPTOMS

This is currently one of the most controversial diseases, as it is often, mistakenly, referred to as feline AIDS. It is true to say that there are similarities between feline leukaemia virus (FELV) and human immuno-deficiency virus (HIV); the FELV virus breaks down the cat's immune system, and is transmitted by prolonged exposure to an infected cat's saliva and/or blood, usually while mating. For this reason, many owners of stud cats insist on a recent FELV test for any visiting queens.

In certain ways, the chemical structure of the two viruses are similar; indeed, some of the early inroads into finding an antibody to HIV were achieved by examining the FELV virus, as more was known about it than AIDS. Here the similarities stop and it must be made clear that the two viruses are not interactive or transmissible.

ACTION

The symptoms for FELV vary because of the nature of the virus. A cat does not die of FELV, but of whatever illness it develops due to the breakdown of its immune system. Persistent infections will probably cause your vet to investigate further, and a simple blood test will reveal whether or not the virus is present. If the test proves positive, the cat will be retested a fortnight or so later. It is quite possible for a cat to register positive, indicating that it has had recent contact with the virus, then after a fortnight, to register negative, showing only a transient FELV infection.

As research continues on the FELV virus it is important to talk to your vet, who will be able to give you all the recent information. Remember that it is not a death sentence for your cat if it proves to be positive; however, if you have other cats that are negative it would be sensible to rehome it to a cat-free household, where it will probably live on to advanced years, but without the possibility of infecting other cats. Like most viruses, FELV cannot live for long outside a feline host and is killed by most disinfectants.

VACCINE

Although a FELV vaccine has been available in the USA, it is only since the beginning of 1992 that a vaccine has been licensed for use in the UK. Vaccination is a two-stage process with inoculations administered fifteen to twenty-one days apart. It is advised that only healthy FELV-negative cats should be inoculated and before inoculation your cat should be tested to be sure that it is negative. FELV-negative queens should be inoculated before mating; pregnant cats should *not* be inoculated.

You cannot catch AIDS from a cat that is FELV positive any more than your cat could acquire AIDS from a person who is HIV positive.

• RABIES •

DESCRIPTION/SYMPTOMS

This is one of the killer diseases and, unlike most animal infections, is transmissible to man – often with fatal consequences. For this reason, all rabies-free countries enforce a quarantine period for the import of live-stock from territories where the disease exists. Hydrophobia is the clinical name for rabies, and describes the ultimate symptom – fear of water. A change in temperament is often the first sign; a usually quiet and docile cat may suddenly, without provocation, become aggressive. It may foam at the mouth and in later stages suffer from paralysis, especially of the jaw.

ACTION

Once an animal has contracted rabies, there is little that can be done for it. If rabies is suspected, it is imperative to contact your vet for a confirmed diagnosis; the local authority and the police will have to be notified. The disease is transmitted by saliva and other body fluids, which contain a high concentration of the virus. This means that a simple lick from an infected animal into a small open wound on a human poses just as much risk of transferring the infection as an actual bite from the animal.

VACCINE

Most countries with endemic rabies insist that all animals capable of carrying the disease are immunized against it. There are certain island nations, for example the UK and New Zealand, which are rabies-free zones at present. In the UK, the government policy is not to inoculate against rabies, except for animals that are to be exported, although this could well change with the opening of the Channel Tunnel.

• FELINE INFECTIOUS PERITONITIS •

DESCRIPTION/SYMPTOMS

When the feline infectious peritonitis (FIP) virus was first discovered, it caused widespread anxiety. It is extremely difficult to diagnose, because of the variety of associated symptoms, and a positive diagnosis can usually only be made from a post-mortem; by this time it is somewhat late to help the poor cat. At first, it was thought to be highly infectious and it put terror in the heart of many a cat breeder.

There appear to be two kinds of FIP, wet and dry. Classic FIP manifests itself by way of a swollen abdomen as the peritoneum (the membrane lining the cavity of the abdomen) fills with fluid. This is accompanied by general ill health, diarrhoea, vomiting and weight loss. The dry form affects the nervous system and is usually harder to detect as the symptoms are similar to those of many other ailments. These include jaundice, respiratory problems, loss of coordination and, in the final stages, fits.

ACTION

Recent research shows that FIP is not as infectious as was first thought. FIP is one of many corona viruses; although it is possible to take a blood test and establish the titre level (concentration) of these viruses in the blood, it does not give much information as to which particular corona virus the cat has been exposed to. It is important that no cat is put down simply on the result of a positive corona virus (titre) blood test. It is now thought that FIP is mainly carried in an infected cat's saliva; it cannot live long outside the feline host and is killed by most veterinary disinfectants.

VACCINE

To date, there is no inoculation available for FIP but, as veterinary science progresses every day, there may well be a vaccination available soon.

• CHLAMYDIA •

DESCRIPTION/SYMPTOMS

Only recently has chlamydia been isolated as a distinct virus. The symptoms can be very similar to those of severe cases of cat flu – usually severe discharges from the eyes and nose. It is not a common infection, and is generally found in multi-cat breeding households.

ACTION

Take the cat to the vet for the correct diagnosis. If it is chlamydia he will administer a course of antibiotics. It is important to keep the cat's eyes moist to prevent adhesions forming between the inner eyelid and cornea and the vet will prescribe a suitable medication. If the cat is part of a multi-cat household, it will have to be isolated.

VACCINE

In the UK, a vaccine has been developed, and has been licensed for administration by veterinary surgeons since 1991.

PARASITES

There are two main kinds of parasitic infestation: internal and external. Both cause distress and discomfort and, if left untreated, can result in illness. The earlier the signs of infestation are spotted, the sooner they can be treated. If you suspect any of the following may be present in your cat, take it to the vet as soon as possible.

INTERNAL PARASITES

◆ WORMS ◆

DESCRIPTION/SYMPTOMS

At some time during its life, almost every cat gets worms. There are two kinds: round-worms and tapeworms. They can be avoided by worming the cat regularly; suitable preparations can be bought from the vet.

Roundworms live in the intestine, feeding on partly digested food. This means that the cat is not receiving all the necessary nutrients from its diet, and will look out of condition with a dull, starey coat, and may have a pot-bellied appearance. In a young kitten, the results can be more dramatic than simple loss of condition: diarrhoea, constipation and anaemia may well occur, making the cat seriously ill. The roundworm's eggs are passed out in the faeces, and can lead to re-infestation without attention to hygiene.

Tapeworm infection is usually identified by the presence of what look like wriggly grains of rice around the anus; these are the ripe sections of the tapeworm containing the egg. Fleas act as an intermediate host in the tape-worm's life cycle: the flea eats the egg, the cat eats the flea, and the egg is released into the intestine for a new cycle to begin. For this reason it is also important to deflea your cat.

ACTION

It is possible to 'worm' your cat for both varieties with one pill, but this may not be suitable in all cases. Your vet will advise you of the most appropriate preparation, the dose to be given and the frequency with which the course should be repeated. If you do buy a preparation from a shop, make sure you read the instructions clearly before administering to your cat. However, proprietary brands are rarely as effective as those the vet can supply on prescription.

◆ TOXOPLASMOSIS ◆

DESCRIPTION/SYMPTOMS

Although not strictly a parasitic infection, this condition causes much publicity and concern. It is a protozoal zoonosis, which means that it is a disease communicable to humans from animals, particularly, in this case, from cats and dogs.

ACTION

Toxoplasmosis rarely causes illness in cats, or indeed in adult humans. The real risk is to the unborn human embryo where, in extreme cases, it could cause a deformity such as blindness. The eggs from toxoplasmosis are excreted in concentration in the faeces of infected cats; for this reason it is important for pregnant women to avoid handling litter trays. Likewise, ensure that children wash their hands after handling the cat and especially after performing litter tray duties.

EXTERNAL PARASITES

Any cat allowed to go outside will meet with an assortment of external parasites all dying to get stuck into a feline host.

BELOW
The most obvious reason for a cat to scratch is simply to relieve an itch, as this cat is demonstrating. However, if a cat persistently scratches it could be indicative of flea infestation and so it would be sensible to consult the vet so the appropriate treatment can be administered.

• FLEAS •

DESCRIPTION/SYMPTOMS

Fleas are the most common parasite. Found on town and country cats, they are a universal pest.

Usually, the first sign of flea infestation is that the cat starts to scratch a lot, particularly around the back of its head and at the base of the spine. This is most common in the spring and summer, when the warmer weather encourages the fleas to come out of winter hibernation. Unless your cat has a severe infestation, you may not actually see the fleas – they hop very quickly – but it is easy to detect if your cat is infested by examining the fur for the telltale sign of flea dirt, which looks like little black specks similar to coarse-ground black pepper. Fleas are blood suckers and, although their dirt looks black, it is actually digested blood. Put the cat on a clean, white surface that has been dampened and comb through the cat's fur; if the dirt that falls out turns red when it dissolves on the damp surface this is a sure sign of fleas.

ACTION

It is possible to buy flea collars, but they are rarely effective and can sometimes cause an allergic reaction around the neck. Flea powders and sprays bought from a store are usually equally ineffective; go to the vet and buy a good-quality product which will effectively rid your cat of these pests. It is also possible to buy a preparation for treating your home and furnishings. Always read and follow the instructions correctly.

Regular spraying of your cat and its bedding, especially during the summer, should ensure that fleas do not become an endemic problem in your home. For every flea on a cat, there can be 200 living in the house waiting their turn to jump on the cat, feed, hop off, breed and multiply. Remember that fleas are quite partial to human blood too, but will only stay long enough to have a quick bite; we do not have the invitingly furry bodies that encourage fleas to take up permanent residence.

• MITES •

DESCRIPTION/SYMPTOMS

There are basically two kinds of mites: those that attack the fur, and those that live in the ears. Mites themselves are, as their name implies, minute and cannot be detected by the human eye; it is the damage they cause that can be clearly seen.

Fur mites can cause hair loss, resulting in the scaly, scabby skin condition that is often called 'mange'. An unpleasant thick, brown, waxy, pungent build-up in the ear canal is typical of ear mite infestation.

ACTION

Mange can look quite similar to ringworm, so the cat should be taken to the vet for correct diagnosis and treatment. For ear mites, you can gently clean the outer area of the ear with a cotton wool swab or cotton bud, but extreme caution must be used as the ear is easily damaged. Your vet will have to see the cat to prescribe the right kind of ear drops, so it is best to leave the cleaning to him, too.

• TICKS •

DESCRIPTION/SYMPTOMS

Ticks are usually found on cats that live in the countryside, where they pick them up from farm animals or long grass.

Like fleas, ticks are blood suckers; however, rather than hopping from one cat to another, the tick buries its head deep into the host's skin, where it remains until it has drunk its fill or is physically removed. A well-fed tick, bloated with blood, can easily be the size of a pea.

ACTION

It is quite easy to remove a tick yourself; the important thing is to make sure that you get the whole tick out, head and all. If the head is left behind in the skin, it will become infected and cause an abscess to develop. The tick has hooks on its head which it uses to attach itself to its host; to get these hooks to relax it will be necessary to anaesthetize the tick with alcohol. If you do not have surgical alcohol handy, use vodka, whisky or gin – more expensive but just as effective. Swab the tick with alcohol and then pull it out with a pair of tweezers. This can be a bit gruesome so, if you are squeamish, take the cat to the vet for him to deal with it.

BELOW *If ear mite infestation is suspected, the vet will make a detailed inspection of the ear canal.*

Inevitably, at some time during your cat's life you will have to administer a pill to it. Cats do tend to wriggle, but with a little practice it is not too difficult a task. It is most important, especially if the pill is part of a course of antibiotics, that you ensure the whole pill has been taken.

HIDING THE PILL

You can try concealing a pill in food so the cat takes the medication without

realizing it. Do not crush it up and mix it in the cat's meal as some of the food and pill may remain uneaten. Use a small piece of favourite food, such as minced chicken or fish, crush the pill and mix the two together to something the size of a walnut. Make sure the cat eats it all, and you will know that it has also taken the medication. Many cats love butter: again, crush the pill and mix it with a small amount of soft butter; put on the top of one of the cat's paws and you will find it will lick it all off.

GIVING A PILL BY HAND

The obvious way is to open the cat's mouth and put in the pill, but this is not as easy as it sounds. Some cats are extremely clever at hiding pills in their mouths, then spitting them out when you are not looking. With practice, the following method is the simplest:

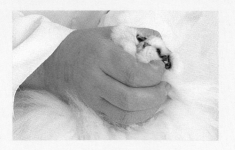

1 To open the mouth, place your hand over the cat's jaw, holding the head back; with thumb and forefinger on either side, push on the cheeks and the mouth will open.

2 With your other hand, quickly shoot the pill as far back in the throat as possible.

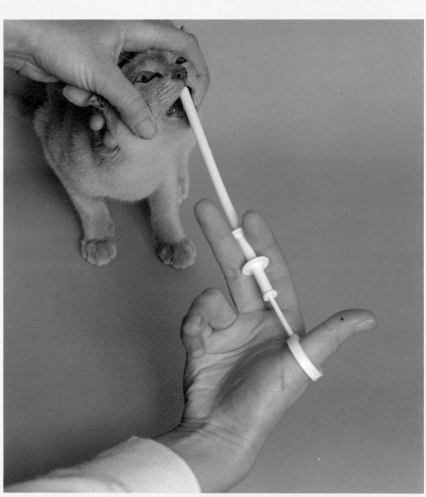

PILL POPPERS

It is possible to buy a gadget known as a 'pill popper' (see above). This is a long plastic plunger which looks a bit like a cake icing syringe. Load the pill, open

the cat's mouth, insert the popper, and push the plunger. This shoots the pill to the back of the cat's mouth. Close the mouth and nostrils as in the method described right.

3 Shut the mouth, and keep it closed with one hand, while closing the nostrils with the other – this forces the cat to swallow. When you have seen the cat swallow, release your hands. The pill has been administered.

AILMENTS AND ILLNESSES

In general, the feline species is a healthy one. Your cat, regularly inoculated, well fed and cared for, should live a good life. However, there are various infections to which it may succumb. Most of these can be cleared up quickly and effectively by correct diagnosis and the administration of antibiotics from a qualified veterinary surgeon; some can be quite effectively treated at home. It is always best to seek veterinary advice, even if only over the telephone. The golden rule is never attempt any treatment unless you are completely confident that you are carrying out the correct procedure in the right way.

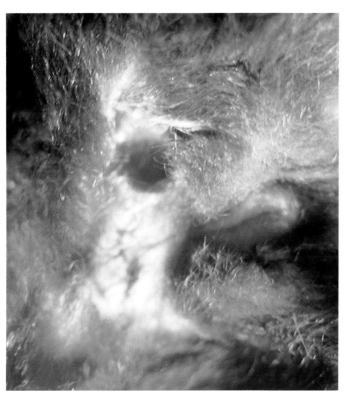

• ABSCESSES •

DESCRIPTION

An abscess is most likely to form following a bite from another cat, but this is not always the case. Any untreated puncture to the skin can become infected, causing an abscess. Diagnosis is not difficult; an abscess looks very much like a large pimple which, in effect, is what it is – a pus-filled lump sited at the point of the wound.

ACTION

It is important to clear the infection as soon as possible to prevent septicaemia setting in; the cat should be given a course of antibiotics immediately. Applying a hot compress will help to burst the abscess and evacuate the pus. Afterwards, the open wound must be kept clean to stop the abscess reforming; applying a wad of cotton wool soaked in warm, dilute, saline solution is effective.

• ACNE •

DESCRIPTION

Feline acne is most commonly seen on the chin of a cat that lives in a single-cat household. It is not easy for a cat to reach this part of its face. Without the aid of a feline friend's rasping tongue to clean away the greasy remains of a meal, the pores are likely to clog up, forming blackheads. These may become infected and cause acne which, if severe, can result in an abscess (*see left*).

ACTION

The application of cotton wool soaked in warm saline solution will help the acne to come to a head and burst; follow up by applying a mild antiseptic suitable for cats. If the condition persists, contact your vet; it responds well to antibiotics.

• ANAL GLANDS •

DESCRIPTION	ACTION

On either side of the anus are two small openings which lead directly from the anal glands. Because of their situation, it is possible for these openings to become blocked, causing an infection to set in in the glands. Normally, these openings are almost imperceptible; when blocked they are more obvious and look like two black grains of rice on either side of the anal sphincter. The cat may drag its bottom along the ground, or indulge in frequent washing of the area, obviously trying to relieve an irritation.

The blockages can be removed, with care and in a very docile cat, by quickly pulling them out with fingers or a pair of tweezers. This should never be attempted with a strange cat, or if you do not know what you are doing. Treatment of infected anal glands is best left to your vet, but it is possible to express them yourself. Apply a hot cotton wool compress and gently squeeze from each side. The exuding matter will smell pungent and, if you do not have a strong stomach, the process is best left for the vet to carry out. Untreated, the infection may result in an abscess which, in this sensitive area, is extremely uncomfortable for a cat.

• ANAL PROLAPSE •

DESCRIPTION	ACTION

This is not particularly common, but once seen is never forgotten; it looks dramatic, and will cause many owners to go into a panic. Anal prolapse is when a small section of bowel turns inside out, with the result that the cat looks as if it has a raspberry protruding from its back passage.

It is important to get the cat to the vet as soon as possible as it will be in great discomfort, and may well need surgical attention. The main cause of anal prolapse is an unbalanced diet without adequate roughage, although there are other reasons. Your vet will advise you. Never attempt to push the bowel back into the rectum yourself.

• ARTHRITIS •

DESCRIPTION	ACTION

This is most common in the older cat but, as with human arthritis, it can strike at any age. In younger cats, it can be related to calici virus, one of the forms of cat flu, and is usually transient. Arthritis affects the skeletal joints, resulting in swelling, inflammation, pain and (if in a limb joint) lameness.

Contact your vet for a correct diagnosis, and discuss which of the treatments currently available are most suited to your cat. Heat is a great soother, and a hot water bottle or heated pad will give much relief to this painful complaint. Massage is often beneficial, but should be administered with care; there are many electric massagers available commercially. Applied correctly, these can alleviate some of the pain and increase mobility in the affected limb. Osteopathic manipulation is sometimes used. Arthritis can be encouraged by obesity, so it is a good idea to keep your cat at the right weight for its size and build.

LEFT
Any cat suffering from arthritis will benefit from additional heat, and a heated cat bed will help tremendously.

• ASTHMA •

DESCRIPTION	ACTION

Cats can show allergic reactions to many environmental agents, and these cause the respiratory distress commonly called asthma. The symptoms can be snuffles, sneezes, weeping eyes and difficulty in breathing, but these could equally be indicative of cat flu.

It is important that your vet examines the cat to make the correct diagnosis. If he thinks asthma is the cause, he may suggest that the cat is confined indoors, with the windows closed, when the pollen count is high.

ABOVE
Just like humans, cats can suffer from allergies such as asthma and hay fever. If your cat is prone to this, it is wise to keep it confined indoors when the pollen count is high.

BELOW
If an allergic reaction causes irritation to the eyes, the vet may well suggest the application of a soothing eye ointment; never administer a preparation that is not recommended by the vet.

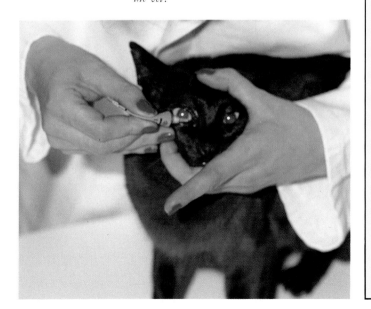

• CONSTIPATION •

DESCRIPTION

Constipation is usually caused by an unbalanced diet, and so can quite often be cured by adding roughage to the food, such as bran. A constipated cat will typically have an 'open' (out of condition) coat, appear lethargic and will strain on its litter tray without passing a motion. The occasional hard stool may be blood-spotted, caused by a ruptured capillary.

ACTION

A constipated cat may be treated at home by giving it a little liquid paraffin. If symptoms persist, consult your vet as there may be a more serious underlying cause, such as an intestinal blockage caused by fur balls.

• DANDRUFF •

DESCRIPTION

This is not a life-threatening problem, but does look unsightly. Dead flakes of skin, or dander, build up in the fur and tend to accumulate if the cat is not regularly groomed. Dry skin can aggravate the situation, and this may be caused by diet, so a change to a more oily food such as sardines or pilchards may help to clear it.

ACTION

An application of fur-conditioning lotion will give a rapid, but temporary, improvement. If the condition persists, there may be a dermatological problem for which your vet will be able to prescribe suitable treatment. Also consult your vet if you find yourself with a skin rash on your chest or arms, as this may be an indication of skin mite infection transferred from the cat.

• DIABETES •

DESCRIPTION

This can affect a cat at any age, but is usually seen in older or overweight animals. The symptoms are an increase in thirst and appetite, but with marked loss of weight. Your vet can make a confirmed diagnosis of this condition after blood and urine samples have been analyzed.

ACTION

Treatment of diabetes, as with humans, is with daily injections of insulin; your vet will show you how to do this and, once you have mastered the technique, it is not difficult. It is important that a diabetic cat receives meals at regular intervals, and that the diet should not contain carbohydrates or sugar. Once the treatment has begun and the condition stabilized, there is no reason why the cat should not live for many years providing the correct medication and modified diet are followed.

• DIARRHOEA •

DESCRIPTION

Many cats have the occasional loose motion. In most cases, this is caused by eating something too rich, or perhaps not as fresh as it should have been.

ACTION

Starve the cat for twenty-four hours, giving it only still mineral (not tap) water to drink, and a teaspoon of plain, live yoghurt three times a day. This will help to readjust the natural bacterial balance in the intestine. If the diarrhoea persists for more than forty-eight hours, or the condition worsens, seek the advice of your vet.

• EAR PROBLEMS •

DESCRIPTION

If a cat starts to scratch its ears, or holds its head to one side, there is probably an ear problem. The most common cause is ear mites (see 'Parasites'), but it could be that a foreign body has entered the ear canal, such as a grass seed, which, if it germinates, will cause extreme irritation and discomfort.

ACTION

Seek veterinary advice for correct diagnosis and treatment.

• ECZEMA •

DESCRIPTION

The problem with eczema is that, although it can have many different causes, the outward manifestations of the disease are the same, which makes diagnosis and treatment difficult.

ACTION

Flea allergy is the most common cause of eczema, and the treatment for this is obviously a good dose of flea spray, and regular spraying of the house to ensure that fleas do not continue to breed. Miliary eczema may be caused by a hormone imbalance, often caused by a female kitten being spayed at too young an age for the endocrine system to have fully developed. If this is the case, the cat will be treated with hormone replacement. Certain foodstuffs, just as with humans, can cause an allergic eczema, and this can be treated by a change in diet. Any hair loss with accompanying bald, scaly patches should be investigated by the vet as it could be ringworm (see 'Parasites'), which is highly contagious.

LEFT
An example of flea allergy (dermatitis). The area has been shaved; it would normally show sparse, broken hairs.

• FELINE DYSAUTONOMIA •

DESCRIPTION

This is a relatively recent discovery, originally known as Key-Gaskell syndrome. As one of the main symptoms is a dilated pupil, in one or both eyes, it has also been called dilated pupil syndrome. Other symptoms may include vomiting, constipation, along with dryness of the nose and mouth causing gagging and difficulty in eating.

ACTION

Research still continues into this condition. At present it is not known how contagious it is, how it is transmitted or how it is caused. Treatment can, therefore, only be symptomatic. It usually affects younger cats, although it has occasionally been seen in older animals, and it has a high mortality rate.

ABOVE
If feline dysautonomia is suspected, the vet will examine the eyes carefully checking the reflex responses of the pupils.

• FELINE INFECTIOUS ANAEMIA •

DESCRIPTION

For some reason feline infectious anaemia (FIA) seems particularly to affect young male cats. It is a bacterial infection and is thought to be transmitted by flies and mosquitoes. Symptoms include lethargy and loss of appetite, and those normally pink-coloured areas such as the lips, gums and mouth will be noticeably pale.

ACTION

The disease can be confirmed by blood analysis and, if this is the case, further tests for FELV will be carried out. If only FIA is present, and is diagnosed at an early stage, it is treatable; if it is combined with FELV the prognosis is not so optimistic.

FITS

DESCRIPTION

You will be in little doubt if your cat is having a fit; it will fall over, salivate and probably twitch.

ACTION

This requires immediate veterinary assistance, as a fit can have many causes, all of which require immediate attention. If you suspect that your cat has swallowed some form of toxic poison, act quickly. Make up a strong solution of salt and water. Force it down the cat's throat to make it sick; this will get rid of as much poison as possible from the stomach before it becomes ingested. *Never* induce vomiting if a caustic substance is the suspected poison. If you have to handle a cat while it is having a fit, protect yourself with thick gloves and wrap the cat in a towel or blanket.

BELOW
If your cat suffers a fit, protect yourself by wearing thick gloves and wrap the cat up firmly in a blanket.

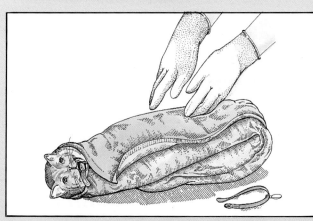

• FUR BALLS •

DESCRIPTION

Cats are very clean creatures and spend much of their time in personal and social grooming. This leads to a certain amount of fur being swallowed. Fur is indigestible and, if quantities are allowed to build up in the intestines, a blockage known as a 'fur ball' will result. Fur balls will probably make the cat cough and may well cause discomfort and constipation.

ACTION

In the wild, a cat would rid itself of fur balls by eating grass, which acts as a natural emetic. Modern housebound cats may need to have hair balls expelled with a dose of liquid paraffin – in an adult one teaspoon, twice a day, for three days, and less for a kitten. The prevention is to groom your cat regularly with a brush and comb, so there is less fur to be swallowed.

HAEMATOMA

DESCRIPTION

A haematoma looks very much like an abscess (a large fluid-filled swelling), but a haematoma is filled with blood and not pus. It is usually seen on the ear, often as the result of a cat fight.

ACTION

The ear is a delicate organ and, if this condition is left untreated, can result in a permanent 'flop' ear. The cat should be seen by the vet as soon as possible if this is to be prevented, and it will also need a course of antibiotics to stop infection setting in.

TOP
A haematoma – a large blood-filled swelling – is usually seen on the ear and is frequently caused by cat fights.

ABOVE
If the haematoma is left untreated the ear will develop a deformity known as flop ear. Immediate veterinary treatment will prevent this.

• MOUTH PROBLEMS •

DESCRIPTION

Usually the first indication that the cat has a problem with its mouth is when it starts to claw at its face or seems interested in food but is unwilling to eat.

For a kitten of around sixteen weeks of age, this is most likely to be part of the teething process. As the adult teeth develop, they push the first teeth out, which can cause the gums to become sore. Occasionally, an adult tooth will not come down straight, resulting in two teeth appearing side by side.

There may be other reasons your cat's mouth is painful. It may have a foreign body stuck in its throat, such as a splinter of bone, a needle, or some other sharp object. Gum disorders, such as gingivitis (inflammation of the gums), will cause severe discomfort, as will a loose tooth. Although these conditions are most common in older cats, they can happen at any age, especially if the cat has not been provided with something crunchy in its diet to adequately exercise the teeth and gums.

ACTION

If your kitten suffers severe teething pain, consult your vet; gum salves manufactured for human babies should never be used.

It you suspect your cat has a foreign body stuck in its throat, contact the vet immediately. The blockage will need to be removed as soon as possible to prevent the cat choking.

For gum disorders and loose teeth, a veterinary examination will be needed and, where necessary, teeth will be extracted.

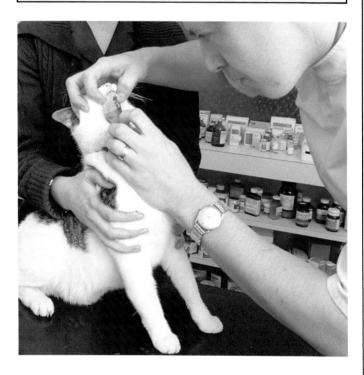

ABOVE
There are several minor gum and teeth disorders that can be treated easily. However, more serious illnesses may be indicated following an inspection of the mouth. For example, paleness in the gums can be indicative of anaemia, possibly feline infectious anaemia (FIA).

• RINGWORM •

DESCRIPTION

This is a very misleading name, as ringworm has nothing to do with worms, parasitic or otherwise. It is an extremely contagious fungal infection, which needs prompt diagnosis to prevent it spreading further, and immediate, often prolonged, veterinary treatment.

The symptoms vary and not all may be present; they are, usually, loss of fur – which tends to break rather than fall out – associated bald spots and sometimes scaly patches on the skin. Head, ears and toes are the most common sites. However, any hair loss should be treated as suspect and the affected cat should be taken to the vet for examination. Diagnosis can be difficult; in most cases ringworm will fluoresce under an ultraviolet Wood's lamp, but not always – some forms of ringworm can only be detected from a culture grown from a skin scraping.

ACTION

Once diagnosed, ringworm is usually treated with Griseofulvin; it may also be necessary to use a fungicidal shampoo. Griseofulvin works by getting into the blood stream and working its way into each individual hair, killing the fungus as it goes. In order to speed up the treatment, some vets clip the fur of longhaired cats – the quicker the Griseofulvin can get to the tip of the hair, the sooner the fungus is cleared out of the system. Some vets also clip the whiskers of shorthaired cats; these are much longer than the close-lying, short fur, and by washing its face the cat could easily reinfect hair that is otherwise clear of ringworm.

An infected cat should be isolated from others in the house-

ABOVE
Ringworm affects mostly the head, ears and feet, but in severe cases can occur anywhere on the body.

hold and it should be kept indoors to prevent infection of neighbouring cats. A strict code of hygiene should be followed: burn all bedding and replace it, following your vet's advice for laundering of the new bedding. As ringworm is one of the few conditions transferable between cats and humans, keep a close eye on you and your family for the formation of scaly, itchy patches; the treatment will be the same, but you will need to contact your doctor for it. Do not allow your doctor to persuade you to put down your cat because you have ringworm – nobody has ever died of ringworm.

After four to six weeks, the vet will want to re-examine the cat under the Wood's lamp, to make sure that all traces of ringworm have been eliminated; if not, a further course of Griseofulvin will be administered. Until your household is cleared, it is inadvisable to visit friends with animals of their own, or for them to visit you, as ringworm can spread on shoes and clothing.

ACCIDENTS AND EMERGENCIES

Accidents happen, even in the most caring homes, and it is best to know what to do in the event of an emergency. A knowledge of feline first aid could make the difference between life and death to your cat. However, if you try to administer first aid, and are not sure of the correct procedure, you could do more harm than good. The chapter on 'Safekeeping of Cats' lists some of the potentially dangerous situations your cat may get into; here we give you basic advice on the immediate actions you can take to help your cat if an accident happens.

● GET TO THE VET ●

For all, bar minor injuries that can be treated at home, apply immediate first aid, if you are confident on the procedure, and then take your cat to the vet immediately. Calling the vet to your home only wastes time, and the chances are that whatever emergency treatment is needed, and this may be an operation, will be available only at the surgery.

If you have to drive the cat to the vet, do not travel alone. If possible, get a friend or neighbour to go with you. Left unrestrained in a carrier, the injured cat may panic and damage itself further. It is better to wrap the cat in a blanket and for someone to cuddle it; this reassures the cat and makes it less likely to go into shock. Also, you are less liable to have a road accident if you know the cat is securely held and as comfortable as possible.

After any accident, it is important to treat the cat for *shock*: keep the cat quiet and warm – wrap it in a towel or blanket – until you can get to the vet's surgery.

LEFT
Cats exerting their territorial rights are quite likely to fight; look out for any sign of a puncture wound, as this could easily lead to infection and the formation of an abscess.

• ANIMAL BITES • (*SEE ALSO* **SNAKE BITES**)

INDICATIONS

Any free-ranging cat will, inevitably, get into a scrap with another cat at some point. The mouths of all animals, including humans, contain many bacteria which, once in the bloodstream, can cause infections.

ACTION

◗ Immediately bathe any wound with a diluted antiseptic suitable for cats, to minimize local infection; even a small puncture wound can result in an abscess.

◗ Next, contact the vet who will give an antibiotic injection immediately, and prescribe the relevant follow-up course of antibiotic pills.

• BURNS •

INDICATIONS

There are basically three kinds of burn, all of which will result in blistering of the affected part:

◗ Contact burns, from direct contact with a hot surface.

◗ Scalds caused by contact with boiling liquid.

◗ Caustic burns from contact with toxic chemicals.

The most likely place for a cat to suffer the first two is in the kitchen. Caustic burns occur more often if a cat wanders into an area where dangerous chemicals are stored.

ACTION

◗ Immediately hold the blistered area under cold running water.

◗ *Never* administer ointments, lotions or butter to the burn.

◗ Do not puncture blisters.

◗ Get the cat to the vet as soon as possible.

RIGHT
If your cat has suffered a burn, immediately hold the blistered area under cold running water until the injury has cooled completely.

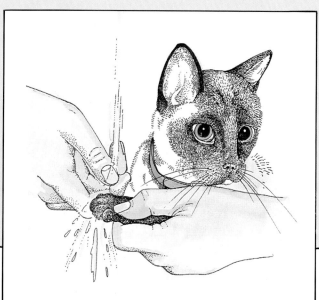

● RESUSCITATION ●

Immediate resuscitation is vital if your cat stops breathing. This can be due to several causes, most commonly *drowning (which includes new-born kittens that have inhaled amniotic fluid) and electric shock (see overleaf).*

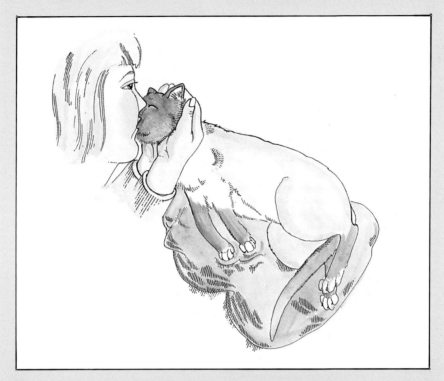

1 Tilt back the cat's head, hold the mouth shut, and blow into both nostrils.

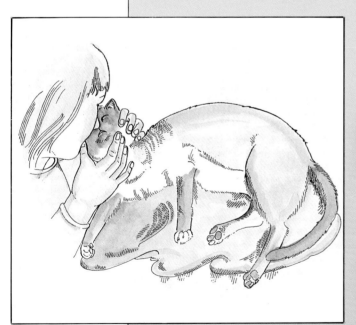

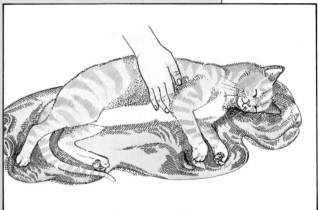

2 Wait until air is expelled and repeat until the cat starts breathing on its own. If the cat still does not breathe, heart massage is needed.

3 For heart massage, lay the cat on its side and rapidly press and then release the area of the chest behind the elbow where the heart is situated. Do not worry how firm you are in treating the cat; if it is not breathing it is, to all intents and purposes, dead. If you manage to revive your cat and it lives, a broken rib is the least of your worries.

• DROWNING •

INDICATIONS	ACTION
A cat does not have to fall into a deep lake to drown; drowning takes place when the lungs become full of water instead of air, and can be caused in many ways. The urgency is to expel this water from the lungs so that the cat can breathe again.	• Hold the cat with its head pointing downward and slap its back firmly. If water is not expelled, and the cat appears not to be breathing, drastic action is called for. • Grasp the cat firmly by the scruff of its neck and by the rear legs, and swing it firmly downwards. • Once the water has been expelled, the process of resuscitation is similar to that suggested by the Red Cross for humans – mouth to mouth – but in the case of the cat mouth to nose is better (see 'Resuscitation').

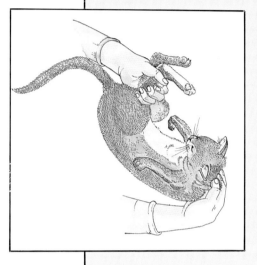

LEFT

To expel water from the lungs, grasp the cat firmly by the scruff of the neck and by the rear legs and swing it downwards.

• ELECTRIC SHOCK •

INDICATIONS	ACTION
Cats are notorious chewers, and the danger of electric cables means nothing to them. If your cat is electrocuted, *do not touch it until you have switched off and disconnected the appliance*, or you, too, will receive a shock.	• Administer resuscitation as described in steps **1–3** (*see previous page*). • Then contact the vet immediately.

• FALLS •

INDICATIONS	ACTION
It is commonly thought that cats always land on their feet, but this is not necessarily so. Fractured jaws are much more common than fractured limbs after falls, and even if a cat has not actually broken or fractured bones, it may be concussed.	• If you suspect a broken bone, get to the vet as soon as possible, restraining the cat to stop it causing itself further damage. • There is also the possibility of internal injury which you will not be able to detect. Treat your cat for shock, and contact your vet who will advise you how to move the cat, then take it straight to the surgery.

LEFT

Cats seem to have a natural fascination for electrical gadgets, and even this seemingly inoffensive telephonel answering machine could cause a nasty shock if the cat chewed through the mains lead.

• INSECT STINGS •

INDICATIONS	ACTION

The most common stings are from wasps and bees. An external wasp sting will cause a localized inflammation. Cats love to chase flying objects and it is not unknown for them to catch and swallow wasps or bees; this may result in them being stung in the mouth or throat.

- For an external wasp sting, soothe the affected area with a cool compress.
- Bees leave their sting behind in their victim, and this must be removed. If you can see the sting, pull it out with a pair of fine tweezers; if not, take the cat to the vet.
- If your cat has been stung in the mouth, you must get the cat to the vet as soon as possible; the throat is liable to swell rapidly and will cause the cat to suffocate if treatment is not administered quickly. In the meantime, put a small ice cube in the cat's mouth to stop the swelling.

• MINOR CUTS AND ABRASIONS •

INDICATIONS	ACTION

A small surface wound can easily be treated at home, just as you would a child's grazed knee.

BELOW
Apply a cold compress firmly to a heavily bleeding wound. If the flow of blood does not stop after a few minutes, take the cat to the vet — the wound may need stitches.

- Apply a little diluted antiseptic and keep a check on it in case it becomes infected.
- Deeper wounds need more attention, especially if profuse bleeding occurs.
- Firmly apply a cold compress directly over the wound to stem the blood flow.
- If this does not stop within a few minutes, take the cat to the vet as the wound may need stitching.

ABOVE
Cats are attracted to small flying objects, but this bee is a potential danger to the inquisitive cat.

• POISON •

INDICATIONS	ACTION

Poisons can get into a cat's system in two ways: ingestion (swallowing), and absorption through the paw pads.

- It is essential to get the cat to the vet as quickly as possible.
- If you know what the poison is, take a sample with you as this will speed up the diagnosis and treatment.
- If you know that the cat has swallowed poison, an emetic by way of a strong salt solution should be forced down the cat in order to make it vomit.
- **Do not make the cat vomit if you suspect that it has swallowed a *caustic* substance, as this will cause even more damage.**

◆ ROAD ACCIDENTS ◆

INDICATIONS

Any cat that has been involved in a road accident will need urgent veterinary help and must be taken to the nearest surgery immediately. There will probably be multiple injuries to treat.

ACTION

◗ Move the injured cat as little as possible.
◗ Next to the cat, lay out a coat, blanket or whatever you have available to use as makeshift stretcher; then gently place the cat on it, moving the limbs as little as possible.
◗ Without allowing it to dangle, support the head just a little lower than the rest of the body; this will ensure that blood is still flowing to the brain and will help prevent brain damage.
◗ Keep the cat as warm and quiet as possible until you reach the surgery.

◆ SNAKE BITES ◆

INDICATIONS

In some parts of the world, snake bites are a relatively common occurrence, especially if you live in the countryside. If you do, you will be aware of the risks, and the snakes that are indigenous to your area. Many people have forgotten that there is still one venomous snake in the UK – the viper or adder.

ACTION

◗ If your cat has been bitten by a venomous snake, it is important to act fast as the venom will spread quickly through the blood system and an antiserum must be administered as soon as possible.
◗ If your vet is many miles away, the best you can do is to apply a tourniquet to restrict the blood flow, and so the spread of venom, but this should only be done as a last resort. It is extremely easy to stop the blood flow to such an extent that the tissue dies, and the limb then may have to be amputated.
◗ If the bite has come from a non-venomous snake, treat as for any other puncture wound (*see* 'Animal Bites').

ABOVE
A cat injured in a road accident must be moved as little and as gently as possible, and it is imperative to get the accident victim to the vet as quickly as possible. A coat makes a handy stretcher; place the cat carefully on the coat and, with another person to help you, take hold of either side of the coat to lift the 'stretcher'. Support the cat's head a little lower than the rest of the body to encourage the flow of blood to the brain.

RIGHT
A cat's pulse can be checked on the inside of the upper-front legs (under the armpits).

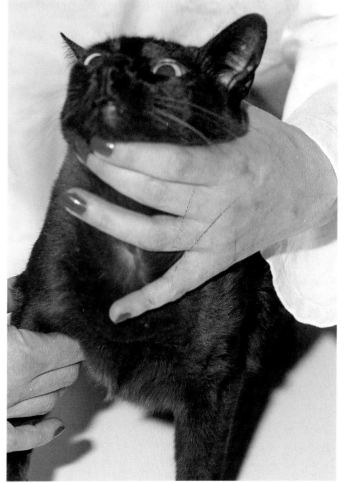

Cat Breed Classifications

Although pedigree cats do not range in size to the same extent as pedigree dogs, there is still a tremendous selection to choose from. Breeds vary, not just in shape, colour and size, but in character and personality too. Some are far more demanding than others, some do not like to be left alone, others prefer to live in a quiet house. Do not be tempted to buy a kitten purely on its looks, or the fact that its colour suits your furnishings. No reputable breeder would sell you a kitten on those terms anyway.

Some cat breeds are old, derived from a natural selection, and may even be unique to a particular region. The tailless Manx cat is a good example of this. More recent pedigree breeds have been genetically engineered by breeders. By introducing new coat colours and patterns and different lengths of fur, breeders have made it possible to find pedigree cats in a kaleidoscopic range of colours.

Cat fancies around the world group pedigree cats in slightly different ways. Some breeds only exist in a few countries, while others are available worldwide. In this book, the pedigree section has been arranged roughly along the lines of the British Governing Council of the Cat Fancy (GCCF) registration system, but detailing alternative names of breeds, where applicable.

There are seven basic groups of cat, each outlined here, or eight if you include the most popular of all cats, the domestic moggie, or non-pedigree.

Longhairs, Persian Type

These all conform to the same standard of points for type, shape, size and length of fur. They all have short noses, little ears and an abundance of fur. They are available in a multitude of colours and patterns. In general, they are quiet, placid creatures that will not demand too much attention. Where they do need extra help is in their grooming; allow at least fifteen minutes a day. If you do not have this time to spare, do not contemplate a Persian cat, no matter how beautiful it may look.

Longhairs, Non-Persian Type

The only factor that these all have in common is the length of their fur. Each breed is unique, both in type and temperament. Within this group are Birmans, Turkish, Maine Coons and Norwegian Forest Cats, to name but a few. There can be no

BELOW
The Birman is one of the most popular of the non-Persian type of Longhair. This pair of Blue-points clearly show the typical restricted coat pattern and the white paws unique to this breed.

generalization as to their characters, as they all are different.

British and American Shorthairs

Like the Persian breeds, these all look basically the same, although there are some differences between the British and American standards. These tend to be quieter creatures than other shorthair varieties, but still need extra grooming because of their thick, short coats. They can grow to be very large and heavy, so if you prefer a small cat, look to one of the other groups.

Other Shorthair Breeds

These are grouped together for convenience. Some varieties, such as the Exotic Shorthair, are actually judged in the longhair section in the UK and there are some longhairs that come into this shorthair category for judging. The group includes all shorthaired cats that do not fit into any other designated shorthaired group. It is similar to the Longhaired Cats of Non-Persian Type section, in that the varieties are all different in appear-

ABOVE
Within the general classification of 'other shorthair varieties' are a myriad of breeds that do not fall into a specific group section. This Egyptian Mau is a spotted cat, but the type is quite distinct from the Oriental Spotted Tabby, a close relation.

RIGHT
For those who prefer a larger breed of cat, the British Shorthair is the answer. Although available in many colours and patterns, the Blue is probably the most popular.

BELOW
As yet unrecognized by the Governing Council of the Cat Fancy (GCCF) in the UK, but popular within the Cat Association of Britain (CAB) and the various American cat fancies, the Snowshoe is one of the newer 'designer' breeds of shorthair cats.

ance and temperament. Included in this group are Abyssinians, Cornish and Devon Rex, American Wirehair and Curl, and the newer varieties such as the Asian cats, including Burmillas, and the spotted Bengals and Ocicats.

Oriental Shorthairs

These are cats of Siamese shape and size, and should conform to the Siamese standard of points. The difference is that they do not display the restricted coat pattern, genetically called the Himalayan factor. They come in a myriad of coat colours and patterns, but are essentially of Siamese temperament.

Burmese

Burmese are a very distinctive grouping, all of the same type and character; only the coat colours vary. They are active cats, need lots of attention, and do not like to be left on their own. In general, however, they are not quite as noisy as Siamese. They have such remarkable characters and loving dispositions that they are one of the most popular breeds of cat today.

Siamese

Siamese are very popular and relatively easily obtained. They are elegant, sleek, and have the most distinctive coat patterns. Like the Burmese, they do not simply need attention – they demand it.

The following chapter describes the details of all these breeds, their character, and the standards needed for a cat to be worthy of a show Challenge or Premier certificate in the UK, or their equivalents in America and Europe (*see Showing Your Cat*).

Before choosing a cat: remember that all cats are first and foremost family pets, so consider the time that each individual breed will require, both for grooming and attention. Your cat is going to be living with you for many years.

LEFT

Siamese are the most instantly recognizable breed of pedigree cat, and one of the most popular. Available in many different colours and patterns, this Blue-point epitomizes the elegance of this enchanting breed.

ABOVE LEFT

The Korat is one of the oldest-known natural breeds of blue cat, and originates from Thailand where it is considered to be 'Si Sawat' – a symbol of good luck. It is only seen in the original blue colour.

RIGHT

The first Burmese, a brown cat called Wong Mau, was imported into the USA in the 1930s. Today, Burmese are available in ten different colours all conforming to the basic standard of points as shown in this pretty young Cream.

GENETICS

Genetics could be considered a science of probability, if a science can be thought of as based on the *possibility* of what could occur and not on precise, proven results. In the mid 1880s George Mendel, an Austrian monk, became increasingly fascinated by the different colours he found among the peas that grew in the monastery garden. He felt there must be some sort of divine order that decided which plants were of which colour and petal shape, which produced wrinkled or smooth peas, and even which were more dwarf-growing than others. What he was really looking at was the outward manifestation (or *phenotype*) of the genetic make-up (or *genotype*) of the plant; this was the beginning of what we now call genetics, which governs both the outward and inward appearance of every living thing – including cats.

Mendel discovered that by selectively pollinating plants with flowers of the same colour, the new plantlets' flowers were nearly always the same colour as the parents'. He continued his research to see if this were also true of animals. For this he selected tame mice, because they breed with great speed, and found again that if two similar parents mated together, the offspring tended to have the same colour as the parents.

However, when two pea plants of different colour, or mice of different coloured coats, produced offspring, the colour produced in the offspring appeared to be dominated by one or other of the parents. Things now started to get interesting: by breeding from two of the same first generation, some of the plants, or mice, resembled one parent and some the other. Mendel had discovered that there are two types of gene, one dominant and one recessive. He had also discovered that all living beings inherit one set of genes from each parent. So how does this basic information relate to cats?

COAT INHERITANCE PATTERN IN CATS

There are many different genes that make up a cat: those for the body, eye and head shape; those for colour, length, and pattern of coat; and even those which can carry a weakness towards certain defects. The combinations can be endless and so in this book I will explain, simply, the coat inheritance pattern.

The phenotype (outward appearance) is dictated by the genotype (genetic make-up), and with the fur of the cat there are three main areas of possibility: longhair or shorthair; differences in colour; differences in pattern.

Coat Colour

As a simple beginning, you could start with two Brown Burmese, both carrying the recessive blue gene. Mate the two together, and each kitten will receive one gene from each parent. The result should be what is commonly termed the Mendelian ratio of 1:2:1 – one brown kitten, two browns carrying the recessive (blue) gene, and one blue. The process is shown more simply in the diagram (*below*), where **D** represents the dominant brown gene and **d** the recessive blue.

This example considers only one set of 'characters', that of coat colour, and so is relatively simple to work out.

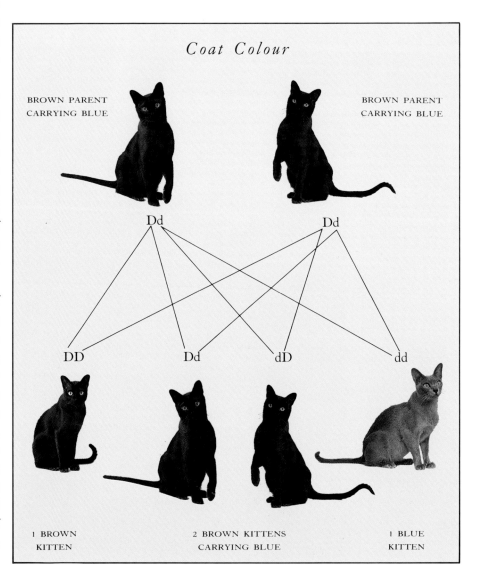

Coat Colour

BROWN PARENT CARRYING BLUE — Dd

BROWN PARENT CARRYING BLUE — Dd

DD   Dd   dD   dd

1 BROWN KITTEN   2 BROWN KITTENS CARRYING BLUE   1 BLUE KITTEN

Coat Length and Colour

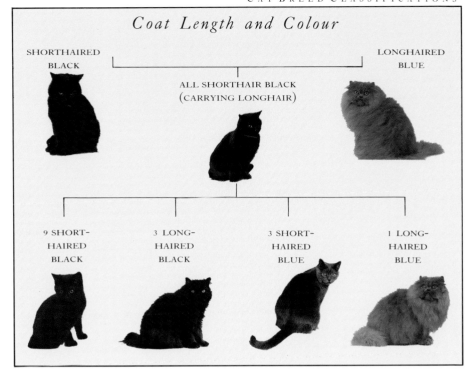

SHORTHAIRED BLACK

ALL SHORTHAIR BLACK (CARRYING LONGHAIR)

LONGHAIRED BLUE

9 SHORT-HAIRED BLACK

3 LONG-HAIRED BLACK

3 SHORT-HAIRED BLUE

1 LONG-HAIRED BLUE

Coat Length and Colour

If you now consider two characters, those of coat length and colour, the possibilities increase. If a shorthaired black cat is mated with a longhaired blue, black coat colour is dominant to blue, and shorthair dominant to longhair. The progeny of the first cross will all be the same. If two of this first cross are mated together there is a possibility to produce four quite different phenotypes, different in both colour and fur length.

The diagram (*above*) shows a ratio of three blacks (dominant) to one blue (recessive) and three shorthairs (dominant) to one longhair (recessive).

Coat Pattern, Length and Colour

Involving a third character, coat pattern, can give rise to even more possibilities.

A recent programme to develop a new breed, the Burmilla – one of the Asian group of cats – shows these three genes, and how they are passed down. The original mating was a Chinchilla male (a longhaired variety with a black-tipped coat) to a Lilac Burmese (a shorthaired, dilute-recessive of unpatterned coat). As the patterned (Chinchilla) gene is dominant to the plain (Burmese) coat, and the

gene for shorthair (Burmese) is dominant over longhair (Chinchilla), all the resultant kittens from this first outcross were shorthaired tipped of Burmese type, carrying the recessive longhair gene.

In theory, if two of these Burmillas were mated together, there are sixteen different colour combinations of coat length and pattern that could result; that is, eight colours with short coats and a corresponding eight with long coats. This comes back to Mendel's idea of ratios between dominant and recessive, and shows how two cats with the same coat colour, length and pattern can produce offspring that look completely different. It also demonstrates how complicated cat genetics become when more than one character has to be considered.

In practice, as breeders wanted to keep the Burmese type, first generation Burmillas were mated back to Burmese, and not to another Burmilla; which explains the relative rarity of the longhaired variety, the Tiffanie, in the early stages of the breeding programme.

This is only an outline for the principles of 'working' cat genetics and how new breeds can be created. In practice it includes much paperwork, research and mathematical calculation.

Burmilla Programme

CHINCHILLA

LILAC BURMESE

*The two breeds selected for the first Burmilla programme mating (**ABOVE**); the first generation Burmilla (**RIGHT**); and (**BELOW**) examples of the variety of coat colour, length and pattern seen in subsequent generations.*

BURMILLA

ASIAN TICKED TABBY

BURMILLA

ASIAN TABBY

ASIAN SMOKE

BOMBAY

CREAM TIFFANIE

LONGHAIRED CATS OF PERSIAN TYPE

Longhaired Persian cats are one of the oldest known breeds of pedigree cat. The long, luxuriant coat gives them a glamorous look and instant appeal. Over the years, the type of the Persian has changed quite radically; today they are a short-faced, compact breed, with a long thick coat available in a myriad of colours.

History

Longhaired cats have been in Europe since the sixteenth century but are known to have existed in certain parts of the world long before then.

The original longhairs were found in Turkey in the region of Ankara and became known as Angoras; these should not be confused with the breed that we know today as the Angora (*see 'Oriental Shorthairs'*). Other longhaired cats were discovered in Persia, modern-day Iran, and because these had more profuse coats, they became more popular.

These early Persians, as they became known, looked quite different from those that we see on the modern show bench. Their faces were much longer and their

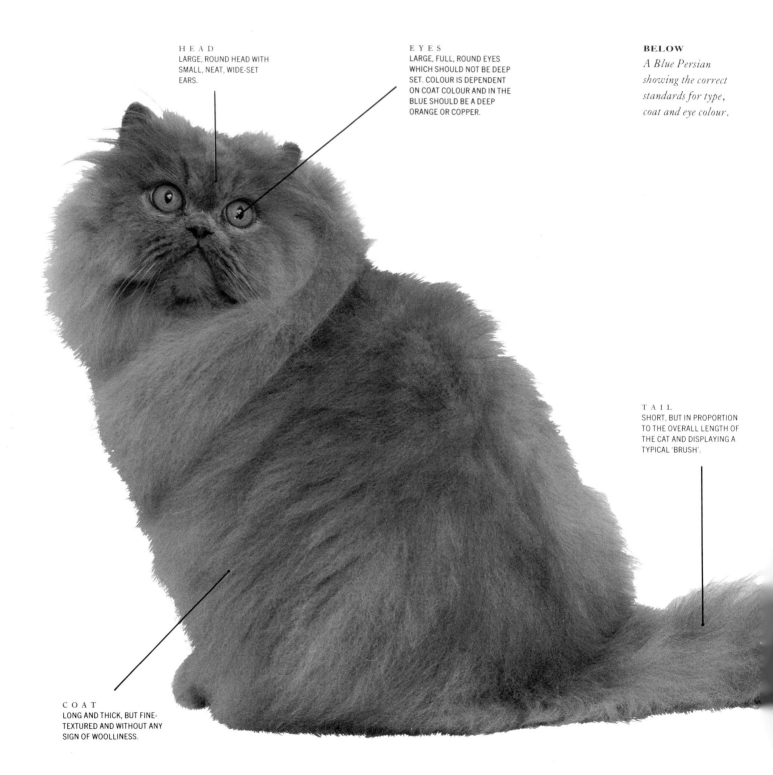

HEAD
LARGE, ROUND HEAD WITH SMALL, NEAT, WIDE-SET EARS.

EYES
LARGE, FULL, ROUND EYES WHICH SHOULD NOT BE DEEP SET. COLOUR IS DEPENDENT ON COAT COLOUR AND IN THE BLUE SHOULD BE A DEEP ORANGE OR COPPER.

BELOW
A Blue Persian showing the correct standards for type, coat and eye colour.

TAIL
SHORT, BUT IN PROPORTION TO THE OVERALL LENGTH OF THE CAT AND DISPLAYING A TYPICAL 'BRUSH'.

COAT
LONG AND THICK, BUT FINE-TEXTURED AND WITHOUT ANY SIGN OF WOOLLINESS.

coats neither as thick nor as luxuriant as their modern equivalents. The earliest record of a longhaired cat was of a brown tabby in the mid-nineteenth century and a solid black about the same time. By the turn of the century, more than twelve different colours were recognized, including what must be one of the most beautiful of all longhairs, the Chinchilla. Today there are more than sixty varieties and colour variations of the Persian.

Character and Temperament

Generally, Persian cats have quiet, gentle dispositions. The time they need for extra grooming is balanced by the fact that they do not demand constant personal attention. On the whole they are not a vociferous breed and will not pine if left alone when you are out at work during the day, although it is always kinder to have two cats rather than one, even if you do opt for Persians.

Type and Standard of Points

Persian cats all conform to the same general standard of points. Only the colour and pattern of their fur differs.

Persians are probably the most glamorous of all pedigree varieties. With long, luxuriant coats, brush-like tails, and a distinctive ruff around the neck, they look quite beautiful but need a lot of grooming to keep their coats in pristine condition. This takes time and any would-be owner of a Persian cat must be prepared to devote at least fifteen minutes a day to grooming their cat.

The standards require a small, elegant, but stocky cat showing large expressive eyes, a tiny nose and small, wide-set ears. The eye colour varies according to the coat colour but should always be complementary. Each colour variation calls for a slight modification in the standards but in general should still give the appearance of a typical Persian cat.

Coat Colours

SELF COLOURS

Black

The Black Persian is one of the oldest varieties and is still one of the most popular. As an adult, the fur should be jet black and the eyes deep copper – a striking combination. Although kittens may show faint ghost markings, or even a few white hairs, these are considered severe faults in an adult. Remember that for any black cat, longhaired or short-haired the full coat colour will take time to develop and so slight variations are acceptable up to about six months of age.

Blue

It is said that the Blue Persian was Queen Victoria's favourite breed of cat. Certainly it is one of the earliest Persian colours and is often thought to be the original colour of the breed (for this reason it is still one of the most popular variations). The coat should be a pale, even blue-grey with no shading or markings, and the eyes should be deep copper or orange.

ABOVE
Historically, black cats have had their ups and downs in the popularity stakes. This Black Persian well illustrates the beauty of the breed, groomed to perfection.

Chocolate

This is one of the newer colours and is a byproduct of the Colourpoint breeding programme, as is the lilac variation. The coat should be an even, solid, medium chocolate-brown, and the eyes a deep copper colour.

Cream

Cream Persians have been known since the end of the nineteenth century, when they were not particularly popular because they were considered to be rather bad, pale examples of a Red.

Today, the reverse is true and they are now admired for their beautiful colouring. It is considered a fault for the cream colour to be too hot; it should be an even pale cream, and the eyes deep copper.

Lilac

This is another variety of Persian from the Colourpoint breeding programme. The coat should be a solid pinkish dove-grey without any sign of masking or lighter or darker patches. The eye colour should be copper.

LEFT
This Chocolate Persian shows the correct warm, medium chocolate-brown colour required.

BELOW
Persian kittens appear so cute and appealing – but do you have the time to spend on their all-important grooming needs?

RIGHT

*The Cream Persian is
one of the best known
of the solid colours of
this breed, and is still
very popular.*

ABOVE

*The Lilac Persian,
like the Chocolate, is
one of the newer colour
varieties and has
arisen by way of the
Colourpoint breeding
programme.*

Red

This may well be one of the older colours of Persian cat but it is one of the most difficult to breed successfully – a common problem when breeding any red- or cream-coloured cat is to produce a coat without any tabby markings. For perfection the coat should be a clear, rich orange colour, solid to the roots. The eyes should be deep copper.

ABOVE AND LEFT
The glamorous look of the Persian belies the fact that it is a sturdy and robust breed that will enjoy outdoor access if this can be safely afforded. An added bonus, Persians will develop a fuller coat if allowed outdoors in the cooler months but, as a minus, will need more grooming!

LEFT
Glamorous White
Persians are still one
of the most popular of
the Persian varieties.

White

The White was the original Angora colour but, as the Persian breed type has been preferred since the beginning of the twentieth century, these white cats no longer bear any resemblance to their Turkish ancestors. They now conform to the typical Persian breed standard, except that they can be found with three different colours of eyes: orange, blue and odd (one blue and one orange). The only extra consideration for White Persians is that their coats may need frequent bathing, especially if they are allowed some freedom outside the house.

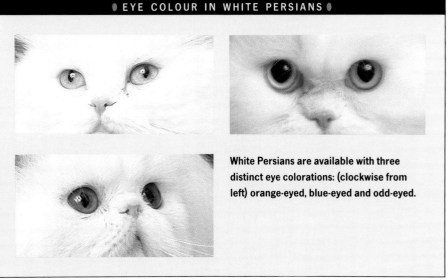

● EYE COLOUR IN WHITE PERSIANS ●

White Persians are available with three distinct eye colorations: (clockwise from left) orange-eyed, blue-eyed and odd-eyed.

RIGHT
*A Blue-Cream
Persian should show a
well-mingled mixture
of pastel tones of blue
and cream.*

*Cameo Persians have
a contrasting coat; the
undercoat should be as
pale as possible with
the tips shading to the
designated colour, such
as Red (**RIGHT**) or
Tortie (**FAR
RIGHT**).*

PATTERNED COLOURS

Bi-colour

These are two-tone cats which may be of
any colour mixed with white. Whatever
the main colour the eyes should be a deep
copper gold. As with any cat that has
white fur, Bi-colours may need to be
bathed occasionally to keep their coats
sparkling.

Blue-Cream

This is a form of the Tortie and so is
usually a female-only variety. As with all
Torties, any males produced are almost
invariably sterile. The Blue-Cream was
developed by mating a Blue and a Cream
together. The standards of the UK require that the two colours are well-
mingled without any obvious patches of a
solid colour. In the USA the reverse is
true and clearly separated areas of definite
colour are required. In either case, the
eyes should be deep copper or orange.

Cameo

These are Persian cats with a restricted tipped coat, related to the Chinchilla and Smoke. There are three densities of Cameo, shell, shaded and smoke, depending on how much tipping appears on each strand of fur. Shell Cameos have just the smallest amount of colour at the end of each hair; shadeds have pigmentation further down the hair shaft, and smokes only reveal white undercoat when the fur is moved or when the cat is walking. For each of these three varieties there are three acceptable colours: red, cream and tortie.

BELOW
Cream-and-White Bi-colour showing the required distinct patches of colour.

Chinchilla

In the USA the Chinchilla conforms exactly to the standards laid down for the Persian breed in general; in the UK the cat is allowed to be more finely boned, with a tendency to a longer muzzle than seen in most Persians.

The Chinchilla is one of the most popular of all longhaired breeds and not without reason. Its white coat, lightly tipped at the edges with black, give the cat a sparkling, almost ethereal and fairy-like appearance.

The coat should be evenly tipped with black on the head, back, legs, tail and flanks; the underpart should be pure white. The nose should be a distinctive brick-red outlined in black. The large expressive eyes should be green, without any trace of blue, with eyelids outlined in black giving an effect of applied mascara.

Colourpoint

(*USA, HIMALAYAN*)

This is a genetically engineered breed, the result of crossing a Blue Persian with a Siamese; this introduced the restricted coat pattern or Himalayan factor. Whatever colour the points, the type should be as for a Persian, but with the colour restricted to the face, ears, tail and legs. However, the eye colour differs to the Persian type in that a deep blue is the required standard for all Colourpoints, similar to that of the Siamese.

Colourpoints are available in just as many colours as are Siamese: seal, blue, chocolate, lilac, red, cream, tortie, tabby and tortie-tabby (torbie). These colours, and the associated colour of nose leather and paw pads, should be identical to those laid down for Siamese (*see 'Siamese' for more details*).

*Colourpoint (USA, Himalayan) Persians show the restricted 'Himalayan' coat pattern that was introduced by mating a Persian to a Siamese, and they are available in just as many colours and patterns as the Siamese. Whatever the colour, it is important for the points to be restricted to ears, face, legs and tail only. The examples shown here are Tortie-Tabby (**RIGHT**), Seal (**BELOW LEFT**), Blue (**BOTTOM**) and Cream (**BELOW RIGHT**).*

Golden

In recent years the Chinchilla has shown that it hides a recessive gene, the red factor. This has given rise to the Golden Persian. The coat should show the same amount of tipping as seen in the Chinchilla, but the base colour must be a rich cream tipped with brown, shading to a lighter hue on the underparts. Just as a Shaded Silver can be produced from the Chinchilla, so can a Shaded Golden; this shows much denser tipping. Both varieties of golden should have vivid green eyes like the Chinchilla.

Pewter

The Pewter is the result of mating a Chinchilla with any one of the self-coloured Persians. Like the Chinchilla, it has a tipped coat but the density of the tipping is much heavier. Deep copper is the required eye colour.

Shaded Silver

This is a more heavily tipped type of Chinchilla, and in many fancies it is not recognized as a separate breed. In general it has similar markings to the Chinchilla, including the brick-red nose and eyes outlined in black; it is only the density of the tipping that distinguishes it.

RIGHT
*Shaded Silvers are a
close relation of the
Chinchilla, showing
the same eye and nose
colours, but feature a
more densely tipped
coat.*

RIGHT
Tabby cats reflect the wild-cat coat pattern that would be needed for camouflage in the wild, but are now bred in many different colours. The Silver Tabby is one of the most popular colours.

BELOW
Persian Smokes can be seen in many colours, but the Black Smoke is the classic. Whatever the colour, the undercoat should be as white as possible with the definite colour most apparent on the back, head and feet. The eye colour should always be copper or orange.

LEFT
This Red-Tabby Persian shows a really full, long and luxuriant coat so typical of this group in general.

BELOW
*Brown-Tabby
Persians are one of the
older tabby colours but
still retain their
popularity despite the
newer, and more
glamorous,
introductions.*

Smoke

This is another variety of Persian that has been seen since the nineteenth century. It was originally bred by crossing a Chinchilla with a Black Persian. The tipping on a Smoke is almost the reverse of that on a Chinchilla; it is only the very base of the coat that shows the pale hue, with the tipped effect taking up most of the length of the fur. Over the years Smokes have been produced in a variety of colours and today ten of these are recognized. Whatever the coat colour the eyes should be copper or orange.

Tabby

Brown Tabbies are possibly the oldest variety of Persian, but as with most things time moves on and even this classic pattern is now available in ten colours: brown, silver, blue, chocolate, lilac, red, and four colours of tortie-tabby (torbie). Because the Tabby conforms to the general standards of Persian, particularly in the profuse coat, it is often difficult to distinguish the tabby markings. Most Tabbies should show deep copper eyes; however, in the silver this colour should be green or hazel.

ABOVE
*Brown-and-White
Tabbies should show
solid black markings
set off against a rich
brown background and
the white area should
be well defined.*

Tabby-and-White

Tabby-and-Whites are accepted in the same colours as Tabbies. They should display even, solid areas of white on their coats and the eye colour should be the same as specified for Tabbies.

Tortoiseshell

Torties are generally recognized as being a female-only variety. The tortoiseshell colour is classically a patched selection of red, cream and black. However, it is possible to have Torties in the recessive and dilute colours of blue, chocolate and lilac. Whatever the colour of coat, the eyes should be deep copper or orange.

Tortie-and-White
(USA, CALICO)

The colour variations are the same as for Tortoiseshell, as is the eye colour. The only difference is that the coat should show solid white patches intermingled with the tortie markings.

ABOVE
*Blue-and-White
Tabbies should have
blue markings against
a beige background.*

LEFT
*Tortoiseshell cats are
most usually a female-
only variety as their
coat pattern is
inherited from a sex-
linked gene. A Brown-
Tortie Persian should
show a coat that has
colours of black, red
and cream.*

BELOW
Exotic Shorthairs are truly cats of Persian type, quite distinct from the British Shorthairs, but with short fur! They are available in all the colours and patterns accepted for the Persians.

ABOVE
Tortie-and-White cats (Calico in the USA) must have at least one-third white in their coat, and the colours accepted are the same as for the tortie colours in general.

EXOTIC SHORTHAIR

I t may seem strange to include a shorthaired variety of cat in a longhaired category. It is an anomaly, but the Exotic is truly a shorthaired Persian; it conforms to all requirements of the Persian breed, displays the same temperament, is available in all the recognized colours for Persians, the only difference being that it has a short coat.

● ADVANTAGES ●

● Sweet-natured and affectionate.
● Not too demanding.
● Good with children.
● Not vociferous; females are quieter than most breeds when on call.
● Within reason, cope with being left alone at home.

● DISADVANTAGES ●

● Require thorough daily grooming.
● Shed fur on carpets and furnishings.

LONGHAIRED CATS OF NON-PERSIAN TYPE

These breeds are all completely different, come from various parts of the world, and many are quite recently developed 'designer' breeds; the only common factor is that their fur is long, but usually neither as long nor as profuse as in the full Persian breeds. Each breed displays its own personality, needs and demands and so must be treated as a separate entity.

ANGORA

(*see Oriental Shorthairs*)

BALINESE

(*see Siamese*)

BIRMAN

History

These are often thought of as the sacred temple cats of Burma, and they originate from this country. They are an enchanting breed and the distinctive coat pattern, with white paws, has given rise to a delightful legend. It is said that a cat, sensing that the high priest was dying, walked over to him and gently put its paws on the priest's frail body to offer companionship during his last hours; as the priest died, the cat's paws were turned purest white and that is how they have stayed to this day. Because of the cat's devotion to the priest, it is further told that each time a Birman cat dies, the soul of a priest accompanies it to heaven.

These tales are charming, but in actuality the breed was probably developed much more recently by crossing a Siamese with a Bi-colour Longhair; this definitely occurred in France in the early 1920s. The first Birmans were of a similar coat colour to the Seal-point Siamese, a pale milky cream with deep seal points and, of course, the distinctive white paws.

Character and Temperament

The Birman is a clever breed, but not as demanding or noisy as the Siamese or Burmese. Their semi-long coats do need extra grooming, but not as much as the Persian Longhairs require. They make ideal pets, and are good with children and other animals.

Type and Standard of Points

The Birman should be a medium-sized cat, with a long, silky coat – although it should never be as long or as dense as the Persian's.

Over the years, Birmans have been bred in many different colours, and can now be seen in twenty variations. The original Seal is possibly the most popular, but the Birman is available in blue, chocolate, lilac, red, cream, and the associated tortie and tabby patterns. Whatever the colour, the coat should be evenly marked with points confined to the face, ears, tail and legs, but with the paws white. These markings must be symmetrical, with the 'gloves' on the front legs ending in a straight line and extending no further than the top of the paws; the rear leg markings, 'gauntlets', should stretch up to the back of the hock. In all Birmans, the eye colour should be bright sapphire blue.

BELOW

Birmans originate from Burma although, unlike Burmese which also come from the same country, they are a longhaired variety. These are Blue-point Birmans.

RIGHT
This Seal-point was the first ever Birman to be made up to the Grand title in the UK. This beautiful neuter boy really displays the finer points required for this breed.

TAIL
SHOULD BE BUSHY AND IN PROPORTION TO THE BODY.

HEAD
BROAD, ROUNDED, STRONG HEAD, WITH MEDIUM-SIZED EARS SET WELL APART. IN PROFILE, THE NOSE SHOULD SHOW A SLIGHT DIP. EYES ROUNDISH.

BODY
MASSIVE, LONG BODY, WITH MEDIUM-LENGTH, THICK-SET LEGS AND LONG SILKY FUR WITH A NECK 'RUFF'.

HEAD
THE HEAD SHOULD BE MEDIUM IN LENGTH WITH A SQUARE MUZZLE AND FIRM CHIN. THE EARS SHOULD BE LARGE AND TALL, SET HIGH AND WELL APART, WIDE AT THE BASE AND TAPERING AT THE TIP.

COAT
THE TYPICAL SHAGGY, WATERPROOF COAT SHOULD NEVER BE FLUFFY. FUR IS LESS DENSE ON THE HEAD, NECK AND SHOULDERS, BUT IT IS IMPORTANT FOR A FACIAL RUFF AND FULL BRUSH TAIL TO BE OBVIOUS.

BODY
LARGE, SOLID AND MUSCULAR WITH LONG, SUBSTANTIAL LEGS AND LARGE, ROUND PAWS.

ABOVE
This Silver-Tabby Maine Coon displays the typical standards of the breed.

CYMRIC
(see Manx, British Shorthairs)

MAINE COON

History

As the name suggests, this was originally an American breed although, in recent years, they have been imported into the UK where they are now becoming increasingly popular. The name comes in part from the state of Maine, where they were first seen, with 'Coon' being derived from the brush-like tail that is reminiscent of a racoon, and so typical of this breed. An alternative, and more romantic, notion is that Marie Antoinette sent her beloved cats to America to escape the French Revolution and these were the ancestors of the modern breed.

The Maine Coon was recognized in some American cat fancies as early as 1967, but it was not until the 1980s that they became popular in the UK, where they are now accepted.

Character and Temperament

Although Maine Coons can grow to be large cats, they have very sweet natures. They are playful and friendly, and make delightful pets.

Type and Standard of Points

The Maine Coon is a large, sturdy, extremely handsome semi-longhaired cat. The head should be long, but not as long as the Siamese, with a definite squared-off muzzle. The legs are long. The coat is heavy and tends to be more prolific around the neck (giving the typical ruff effect), the belly, legs and tail. The coat is not as profuse as on the Persian Longhairs, and does not require as much grooming; however, it is a thick, dense coat that provides the cat with insulation during the cold winter months in New England. The classic Maine Coon is a tabby-and-white, but the breed is acceptable in almost any coat colour and pattern, and the eye colour may be green, hazel, copper, blue, or odd-eyed.

RIGHT
Brown Tortie-Tabby Maine Coons should show black and red markings against a background of warm copper.

LEFT
Tortie-and-White Maine Coons should have a coat predominantly made up of the base colour, with white fur ideally on the face, chest, legs and feet.

RIGHT
*Norwegian Forest
Cats are a new and
interesting breed; they
have the unique ability
to climb up sheer rock
faces, and are both
elegant and energetic.
This Blue Tabby-and-
White typifies the type
required for
this breed.*

NORWEGIAN FOREST CAT

History

This breed is a little similar to the Maine Coon, but developed in the cold climate of northern Scandinavia. The thick coat provided the cat with warmth in severe weather. In Norse tales, legends make reference to a fairy cat, and this may well have been the Norwegian Forest Cat as its plume-like tail has an ethereal look. It is an excellent climber, able to get to areas most cats could not reach, and this has added to the mystique of the breed. It has been seen at shows in Norway since before World War II, but was not recognized by the Fédération Internationale Féline (FIFe) until 1977. The breed is popular in the USA, but has only recently been imported to the UK.

Character and Temperament

The Norwegian Forest Cat is a lively and independent cat. It is a good hunter and, with its thick, waterproof coat, enjoys being allowed freedom in a garden. It does like human company and prefers not to be left alone for any great length of time.

Type and Standard of Points

The head should be roughly triangular in shape, with high-set large ears. The nose should be straight and the eyes an almond shape. The thick, waterproof coat should be long, with long guard hairs covering the dense undercoat.

LEFT
*Norwegian Forest
Cats come in a variety
of colours and
patterns; this is a
Brown Tabby-and-
White.*

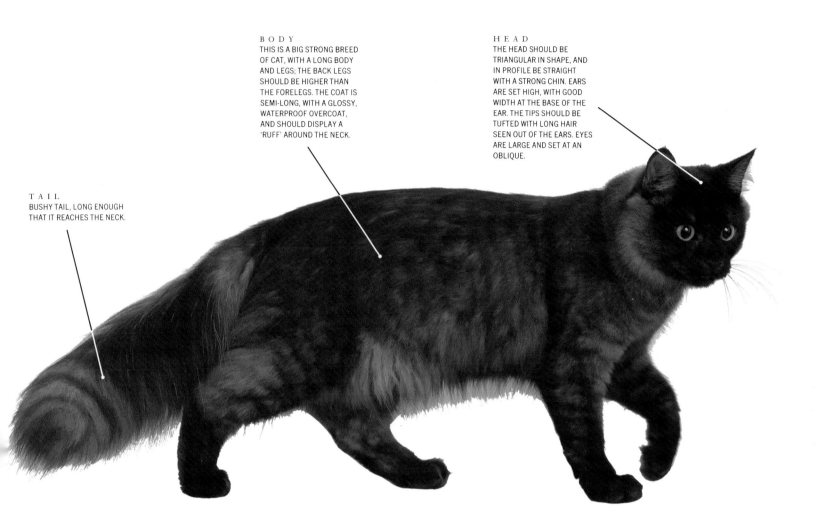

BODY
THIS IS A BIG STRONG BREED OF CAT, WITH A LONG BODY AND LEGS; THE BACK LEGS SHOULD BE HIGHER THAN THE FORELEGS. THE COAT IS SEMI-LONG, WITH A GLOSSY, WATERPROOF OVERCOAT, AND SHOULD DISPLAY A 'RUFF' AROUND THE NECK.

HEAD
THE HEAD SHOULD BE TRIANGULAR IN SHAPE, AND IN PROFILE BE STRAIGHT WITH A STRONG CHIN. EARS ARE SET HIGH, WITH GOOD WIDTH AT THE BASE OF THE EAR. THE TIPS SHOULD BE TUFTED WITH LONG HAIR SEEN OUT OF THE EARS. EYES ARE LARGE AND SET AT AN OBLIQUE.

TAIL
BUSHY TAIL, LONG ENOUGH THAT IT REACHES THE NECK.

ABOVE
This Smoke Norwegian Forest Cat really shows the required 'brush' tail to perfection.

RIGHT
Peke-faced Persians do not conform to the general standards laid down for the Persian breed. They are neither accepted nor bred in the UK, but are available in the USA in as many colours and patterns as acceptable for the Persians.

PEKE-FACED

This is a somewhat controversial breed that is essentially an ultra-type Persian. The breed has been put in this section, as some of the traits it displays are not desirable in the usual Persian type of longhair. The nose is so short as to be almost flat on the face. There is also a very strong indentation between the eyes, giving rise to a typically furrowed brow and causing the eyes to be large and protruding. This is a breed only seen in America, although some ultra-type Persians are bred in the UK, but not to such an extreme. In temperament and character, they are very similar to the Persian Longhairs and, in the fancies where they are regarded as a separate breed, are available in all the colours recognized for Persians.

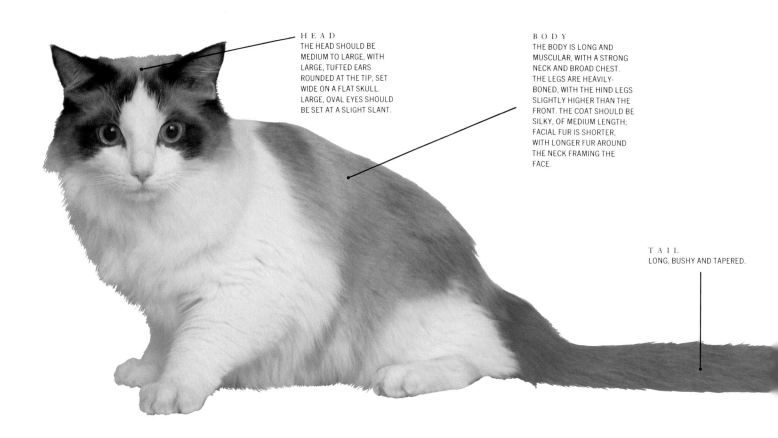

HEAD
THE HEAD SHOULD BE MEDIUM TO LARGE, WITH LARGE, TUFTED EARS ROUNDED AT THE TIP, SET WIDE ON A FLAT SKULL. LARGE, OVAL EYES SHOULD BE SET AT A SLIGHT SLANT.

BODY
THE BODY IS LONG AND MUSCULAR, WITH A STRONG NECK AND BROAD CHEST. THE LEGS ARE HEAVILY-BONED, WITH THE HIND LEGS SLIGHTLY HIGHER THAN THE FRONT. THE COAT SHOULD BE SILKY, OF MEDIUM LENGTH; FACIAL FUR IS SHORTER, WITH LONGER FUR AROUND THE NECK FRAMING THE FACE.

TAIL
LONG, BUSHY AND TAPERED.

ABOVE
Bi-colour Ragdoll, showing the correct 'V' marking on the forehead.

RAGDOLL

History

Much controversy surrounds the history of this breed, which gained recognition in the USA in the 1960s. The charm of the Ragdoll is said to lie in the fact that it will flop in your arms when handled, but this is not uncommon in any cat that trusts its owner.

The first Ragdoll kittens are said to have been born in California to a white Persian queen who had mismated and, after suffering a broken pelvis in a car accident, gave birth to a litter of kittens that flopped when handled. This would be genetically impossible, as the result of a road accident cannot cause the cat's genetic make-up to be changed and so be passed on to future generations. The truth of the Ragdoll's background is open to speculation. Looking at the varieties of Ragdoll accepted today, it is likely that the breed has an ancestry linked with Siamese, Colourpoints or Birmans.

Character and Temperament

The Ragdoll is possibly one of the most laid-back of all breeds of domesticated cats. It is relatively undemanding, very tolerant of most situations, and is gentle and relaxed. It is said that these cats have a lower pain threshold than most, but it is a debatable point, and certainly not one that should be tested.

Type and Standard of Points

There are three basic patterns of Ragdoll that are accepted: bi-colour, colourpoint and mitted, and the colour for each may be seal, blue, chocolate or lilac. The coloured areas are generally restricted to the face, legs and tail, in a manner similar to the Colourpoints' and Birmans' restrictive markings. The fur is particularly long on the chest and abdomen, on the back of the head (giving a distinct ruff), and on the tail, which should be thick and full. The eyes should always be blue.

SOMALI
(see Abyssinian, Other Shorthairs)

TIFFANIE
(see Asian Cats, Other Shorthairs)

TURKISH VAN

History

This is a natural breed of cat which was first discovered around the shores of Lake Van, a remote area of Turkey. The most astonishing fact about the breed is that it not only likes water, but really enjoys going for a swim. It is probably descended from the Angora, one of the original varieties of longhaired cat, and is distinguished by attractive auburn markings around the face and on the tail. Turkish Vans have a distinct white 'thumb print' mark between their ears which the Turkish people call the mark of Allah and so, in their native homeland, these cats are treated with great respect. A trip to modern-day Istanbul will reveal street cats that, although mostly shorthaired, are generally white with auburn markings. In the early 1950s the first pair was brought back to Britain and a breeding programme started; by 1969 they were granted official recognition. Today they grace the show benches on both sides of the Atlantic.

Character and Temperament

Turkish Vans are very friendly, sociable and intelligent, and they like company. They have soft voices, and are happy to live quietly inside your home, as long as they are given attention and the odd game to play. They like to be offered the opportunity for a swim and so, if you do not have a pool, let the cat take some exercise in the bath.

Type and Standard of Points

The classic form of Turkish Van is a chalk-white semi-longhair cat with auburn markings restricted to the head, ears and tail, and with amber eyes. Over the years, various other colours have been noted and the Van is now accepted in both auburn and cream colours, and with amber, blue or odd-coloured eyes. The head is a short wedge shape, with a longish nose, and the ears are large and pointed.

BODY
A LONG, STURDY CAT THAT IS STRONG AND MUSCULAR, WITH MEDIUM-LENGTH LEGS.

HEAD
HEAD SHOULD BE A SHORT WEDGE AND SHOW A LONG NOSE; IN PROFILE, NOSE SHOULD BE STRAIGHT BUT WITH A SLIGHTLY NOTICEABLE DIP. EARS ARE LARGE, SET HIGH ON HEAD AND FAIRLY CLOSE TOGETHER. THE EYES SHOULD BE LARGE AND OVAL.

RIGHT
The Classic Turkish Van has a white coat, with auburn markings and amber eyes.

TAIL
THE TAIL SHOULD BE BRUSH-LIKE AND IN BALANCE WITH THE OVERALL LENGTH OF THE CAT.

BRITISH AND AMERICAN SHORTHAIRS

British and American Shorthairs gain their names from the fact that they are the indigenous breeds of these two countries. Although American Shorthairs probably originated in Great Britain, travelling to America around the time of the Pilgrim Fathers in the early seventeenth century, the two breeds are still very similar with only minor differences required in their standards.

◆ HISTORY ◆

The history of this breed goes back to Roman times and it is thought that the invading Roman troops first brought shorthaired cats to Britain. Written records for the British Shorthair only go back to the turn of the century although it is clear, from old paintings and engravings, that they had been around for several hundred years before this.

Shorthairs were probably originally kept for their mousing ability and for the fact that, unlike the Persians and Angoras also seen at this time, they did not need human help with their grooming. They were a self-sufficient variety, which provided a useful service to man, and it is recorded that most ships setting sail for the New World included several cats on the cargo list.

The oldest recorded type of shorthaired cat was the tabby. Elegantly and attractively marked with darker stripes or spots, the tabby's coat reflects the coat pattern of its wild cat ancestry; the cats worshipped in Ancient Egypt were similar tabbies, although their coats tended to be ticked. On the show bench today, Tabbies are still very popular but the newer, glamorous Silver Tabby is more in evidence than the original Brown Tabby, which seems to have been ignored in the breeding programmes of recent years.

The self-coloured varieties of British and American Shorthairs are among the most popular, the most obvious example being the Blue. They are also available in various other colours and patterns; more recent introductions include the Tipped, showing the coat markings associated with the Chinchilla, and the Colourpoint, a true British cat but with the distinctive restricted coat pattern usually associated with the Siamese.

BELOW

The British Shorthair is essentially a chunky feline, well-illustrated by this orange-eyed White.

Character and Temperament

British and American Shorthairs can grow to be some of the largest domestic cats, but their gentle and shy dispositions have caused them to be described as the 'gentle giants'. They are loving and affectionate, have quiet voices and, rather like the Persians, do not continuously demand their owners' attentions. Generally, they do not seem to have the wanderlust of the foreign breeds and will not mind being confined to an apartment. Even if given the freedom of a garden, they are unlikely to wander far.

Type and Standard of Points

British and American Shorthairs should be large, strong, sturdy and muscular. The male is larger than the female, and more obviously so than in most other breeds. Neuters, especially the males, do have a tendency to obesity, so a close watch should be kept on their diet.

Typically the chest should be deep and broad with short, strong legs and neat, rounded paws. The head should be wide and rounded and in males should show definite jowls. In profile the nose should show a 'stop', and the jaw should show a level bite without any sign of being either overshot or undershot. The ears should be small and set wide apart. In all colours and patterns the coat should be short, crisp and dense but without appearing woolly; the only exception to this is in the Manx varieties.

The overall look for the British is for a chunky, cobby cat without the extreme facial expression of the Persian; it is usually accepted for the American Shorthair to be slightly heavier and in general longer than its British counterpart. The colours available are almost the same as those acceptable for the Persian, with more colours for the American Shorthair than the British.

Coat Colours

SELF-COLOURS

White

Although the coat colour should remain the same – an even, pure white – three different eye colours are acceptable: orange, blue and odd-eyed. In a young kitten, the odd patch of darker colour on the top of the head is permissible; by adulthood any such markings should have disappeared and if they remain, are considered a serious fault.

Black

A glossy, jet black is the required coat colour. Moreover, the colour should be solid to the roots, with no trace of rustiness, tabby markings, white hairs or patches. The eyes should be a deep copper without any trace of green.

BELOW
The British Black is typical of this breed; although the kittens are most appealing, remember that they will grow into very large cats when adult, especially if male!

Blue

This is probably the best known of all the Shorthair varieties; in Europe, it is known as the Chartreux. The coat should be a distinctive blue-grey, without any silver ticking, and the colour solid to the roots. The eye colour should be deep copper, as in the Black.

Cream

An even, pale-coloured cream coat is desired; in practice this is hard to achieve and many cats do show faint 'ghost' tabby or spotted markings. The eye colour should be deep copper.

Chocolate

This should be an even, solid, medium chocolate-brown, and the eye colour should be copper.

RIGHT
The British Blue, showing the required golden-copper eye colour, can grow to be an exceedingly large cat.

ABOVE
British Chocolates are a relatively new colour and, like their Persian counterparts, have arrived by way of the Colourpoint breeding programme.

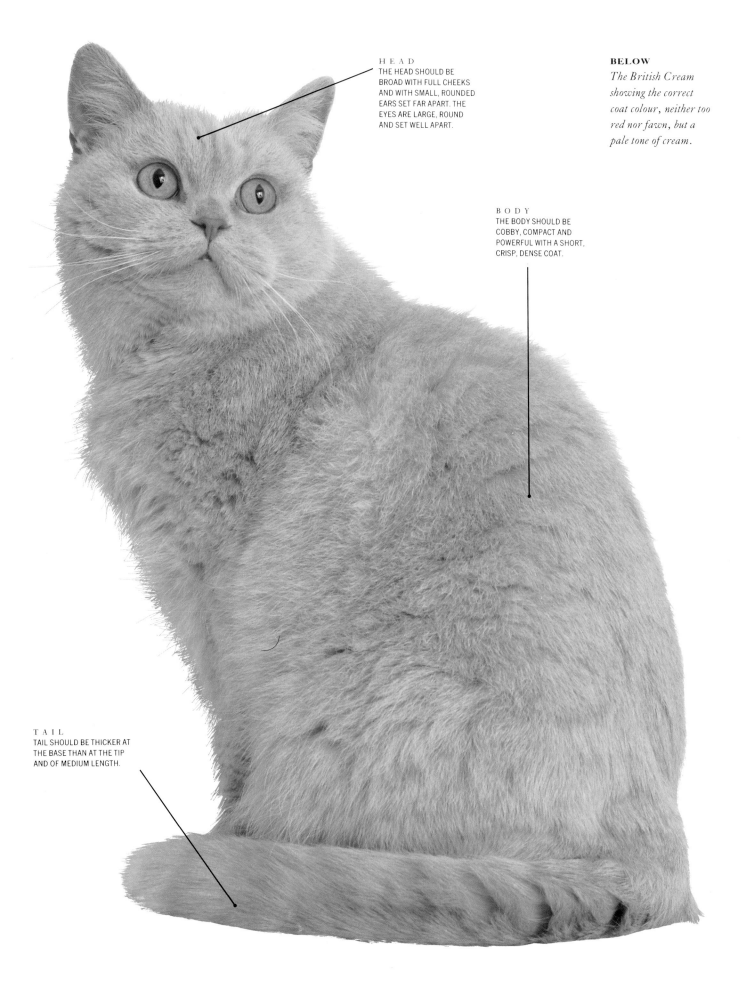

HEAD
THE HEAD SHOULD BE
BROAD WITH FULL CHEEKS
AND WITH SMALL, ROUNDED
EARS SET FAR APART. THE
EYES ARE LARGE, ROUND
AND SET WELL APART.

BELOW
*The British Cream
showing the correct
coat colour, neither too
red nor fawn, but a
pale tone of cream.*

BODY
THE BODY SHOULD BE
COBBY, COMPACT AND
POWERFUL WITH A SHORT,
CRISP, DENSE COAT.

TAIL
TAIL SHOULD BE THICKER AT
THE BASE THAN AT THE TIP
AND OF MEDIUM LENGTH.

Lilac

A solid pinkish dove-grey coat combines with a copper eye colour. The Lilac and Chocolate are quite recent colours, by-products of the Colourpoint breeding programme.

BELOW
Father and daughter of one of the newer colours, Lilac, showing how much larger the male may become in comparison to the female.

ABOVE
The American Shorthair varies slightly from the standards laid down for the British; in general, it is a longer cat and less heavily boned.

◊ TABBIES ◊

British Red Spotted Tabby

American Brown Tabby

British Silver Tabby

PATTERNED COLOURS

Tabby

These are seen in three patterns: classic, mackerel and spotted, and are most often brown, blue, red and silver. Whatever the colour, the markings should be a much deeper hue than the background; for example, Brown Tabbies should have a sable background colour with black markings, the Reds should have a rich red background with distinctively deeper red markings, and the Silver Tabbies a clear silver body colour with black markings. The eye colour depends on that of the coat; in Reds and Browns this should be copper or orange, and green or hazel in the Silvers.

BELOW

Spotted Tabbies are a very popular breed, the Silvers in particular. They should show numerous, well-defined spots throughout the coat.

Tortie

As in the Persian, a well-mingled mixture of colours is desired in the UK, without any solid patch of any one colour. The most popular and most commonly seen of this female-only variety is the Blue-Cream. They can, however, be seen in a variety of colours and the eye colour should be the same as that laid down for the main colour of the coat.

Tortie-and-White

These have been produced by mating a Tortie to a Bi-colour and are seen in the same number of colours as Torties. It is important for the white areas to be clearly defined, and the eye colour should be as for the Tortie.

Colourpoint

This is a more recent colour variation, genetically engineered by breeders. The original cross was between a British and a Longhair Colourpoint, which resulted in early generations showing slightly fluffy coats; this has now been eradicated and Colourpoints today have typical British coats and type. They are available in all the colours seen in Siamese and, unlike most British, have blue eyes.

ABOVE
*A good contrast between the basic coat colour and the points is required for the British Colourpoint, as depicted here in a young Blue Colourpoint (**LEFT**) and Tortie Colourpoint (**RIGHT**).*

LEFT
A Chocolate Colourpoint clearly showing the required coat colour pattern restriction.

● Gentle and affectionate.
● Good with children and other animals.
● Need little extra grooming (except the Manx and Cymric).
● A healthy, sturdy breed.
● Do not mind being left, as long as they have another cat for company.

● Can be prone to obesity, especially when neutered.
● Although very pretty as kittens, can grow into formidable-sized cats.
● Manx varieties need daily grooming.

Tipped

This is a British cat hiding behind a shorthaired version of the Chinchilla's coat. The tips of the fur should be black with pure white underparts, the nose should be brick-red outlined in black, and the eyes should be outlined in black. The Tipped are now bred in a variety of colours, but whatever the colour, the pigmentation should be confined to the extreme tips of the fur only.

Smoke

Effectively the reverse of the British Tipped, the Smoke exhibits a silver undermantle with a denser colour taking up most of the length of the fur. The main colour can be any acceptable for the British Shorthair breed in general. Adults should not show vestiges of tabby markings or any white hair in the coat. Eyes are copper, gold or orange.

Bi-colour

This is a two-tone cat, which can be any of the recognized colours and patterns acceptable for the British, but it must display symmetrical patches of white with the background colour.

ABOVE
The British Tipped is a British Shorthair with the Chinchilla gene introduced to produce the distinctive tipping to the coat.

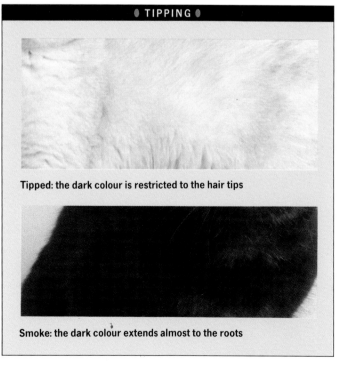

● TIPPING ●

Tipped: the dark colour is restricted to the hair tips

Smoke: the dark colour extends almost to the roots

ABOVE LEFT
This may look like a black cat, but it is a British Smoke; the difference lies in the fact that the undercoat is silver, and not black to the roots.

ABOVE RIGHT
A British Blue Bi-colour; one of many of the colours available for this coat pattern.

RIGHT
The British Bi-colour should have patches of the self-colour and white, with the patches, for perfection, being as symmetrical as possible as seen in this Cream-and-White Bi-colour.

RIGHT
The classic Rumpy Manx has no vestige of a tail and, as seen in this Tortie-and-White, should have a rump that stands higher than the shoulders.

BELOW LEFT
A White Stumpy Manx, showing the distinctive rounded rump required for the breed standards.

BELOW RIGHT
An odd-eyed Tailed Manx, unacceptable for the show bench requirements, but useful to any Manx breeding programme.

MANX
(and Cymric)

The Manx is unlike most British Shorthairs and not just because it usually does not have a tail. The type required for a Manx is less extreme than that required for most British and Americans cats. Also, the Manx nose is usually a bit longer. The coat is accepted in any colour or combination of colours, is thicker and more prone to matting than the classic British Shorthair coat, and for this reason, needs extra grooming.

Manx are generally seen in four forms: Rumpy, Stumpy, Tailed and Cymric. Rumpies have no tail at all and, for perfection, a small dip should be noticeable at the base of the spine where the tail would have been; this is the only type of Manx recognized for showing purposes in the UK, although the other types may be used for breeding. Stumpies have a small amount of tail, more like a bump at the base of the spine, and it is possible to have tailed varieties of Manx too. All Manx cats should have back legs that are considerably longer than the front ones, which gives rise to their typical, rather unusual, rabbit-like gait.

The Cymric is a longhaired variety of Manx and is comparatively rare, especially in the UK. In character and temperament, Manx and Cymric are just like other British varieties and make the most delightful pets.

ABOVE
The Cymric, rare in Britain but popular in the United States, is a longhaired variety of Manx.

ORIENTAL
SHORTHAIRS

*The Oriental is very much an artificially created type of breed.
Although solid-coloured cats of Siamese type have been seen for
many years, usually as the result of a mismating, they were not
popular until the 1950s. Then, experimental matings took
place between Siamese and Russian Blues, among others, and
led the way to the development of the Havana. A byproduct of
this breeding programme was the Oriental Lilac.*

these are available in just as many colours. Genetically, this section could produce an almost unlimited variety of coat colours and patterns.

Character and Temperament

Oriental cats are basically Siamese cats without the restrictive, Himalayan, pattern in their coats. They have exactly the same type and conformation as the Siamese, and their temperament is the same too: outgoing personalities that demand a lot of attention.

Orientals have exceedingly loud voices and will often instigate the conversation – they are not like well brought-up children who only speak when they are spoken to. They want to be involved in every household activity, be it sharing your bed or helping you wash the dishes. Just like dogs, they love to play retrieving games and derive hours of pleasure from a simple piece of screwed-up paper. They do not like to be left for any length of time on their own, and would benefit from a feline companion if you are out at work all day.

Type and Standard of Points

Whatever the coat colour or pattern, the standard requires the shape and type of the cat to be exactly the same as that of the Siamese (*see 'Siamese'*). This means that the Oriental is a medium-sized cat that should feel firm and muscular. It is slender and elegant, but despite its shape and size should feel heavy. Orientals should never be overtly skinny or feel too light in weight.

The eye colour varies to complement the coat colour, and the eye shape should show the typical Oriental slant. The ears should be wide apart and, when viewed from the front, should give the appearance of a triangle from the tip of the two ears down to the point of the nose. In profile, the nose should be straight.

History

Solid colours, other than the original Lilac, soon became possible, and today we have Orientals recognized in ten colours and the associated seven colours of the Tortie.

As the popularity of the Orientals increased, and breeders became aware of the genetic possibilities of different coat patterns, a new programme was started. This gave rise, by mating back to Tabby-point Siamese, to Spotted, Classic and Mackerel Tabbies, in a variety of different colour variations. The Ticked Tabby arrived by crossing a Seal-point Siamese with an Abyssinian. It is equally possible to breed Orientals with a smoke coat, and

ABOVE

The Havana is one of the few breeds of brown cat and is sometimes confused with the Brown Burmese; they are, however, quite different in both genotype and phenotype.

Coat Colours

SELF-COLOURS

These must be of the same colour overall, solid to the roots and without any sign of shading, barring, tabby markings or white hairs. These are some of the colours currently recognized:

Havana

This is a rich, warm brown with brown nose leather and pinky-brown paw pads. The eye colour should be vivid green.

White

A clear, bright white is the required colour, with pale-pink nose and paw pads, and brilliant sapphire-blue eyes.

Black

A solid jet black is required, with paw pads and nose leather the same, and vivid green eyes.

Blue

This should be a light to medium blue, with nose leather and paw pads the same, and the eyes green.

LEFT

The Foreign White should have a pure white, sleek coat and brilliant blue eyes.

RIGHT
*This Oriental Blue
Tortie, one of several
colours of tortie
acceptable for this
breed, shows a well-
mingled mixture of
medium-blue and
cream colours in the
coat.*

Lilac

A pinkish frosty-grey is required, with nose leather and paw pads lavender, and the eyes green.

Other newer solid colours include red, cream, cinnamon, caramel, and fawn.

PATTERNED COLOURS

Tortie

The sex-linked red gene will give rise to the Tortie, which is usually a female-only variety. The usual Tortie is a well-mingled mixture of red, cream and brown, with black and/or pink paw pads and nose leather and with green eyes. Torties can now be seen in several other colours including chocolate, cinnamon, caramel, and fawn; whatever the main colour, it is important for the complementary colours to be well-mingled and the eye colour to be the same as that laid down for the dominant coat colour.

ABOVE
The Oriental Cinnamon is one of the newer colours in this section, and is a warm cinnamon colour.

LEFT
The Oriental Cream should be a cool cream colour, with faint tabby markings acceptable in another good example of the breed.

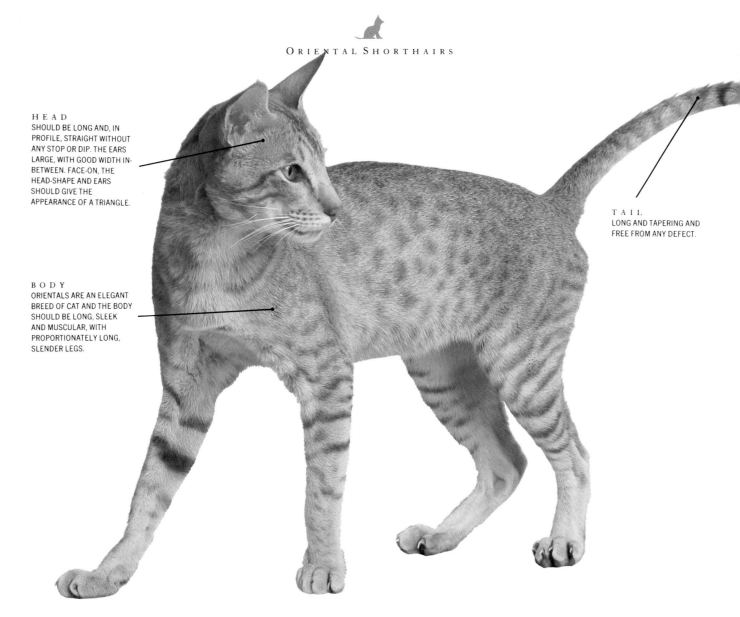

HEAD
SHOULD BE LONG AND, IN PROFILE, STRAIGHT WITHOUT ANY STOP OR DIP. THE EARS LARGE, WITH GOOD WIDTH IN-BETWEEN. FACE-ON, THE HEAD-SHAPE AND EARS SHOULD GIVE THE APPEARANCE OF A TRIANGLE.

BODY
ORIENTALS ARE AN ELEGANT BREED OF CAT AND THE BODY SHOULD BE LONG, SLEEK AND MUSCULAR, WITH PROPORTIONATELY LONG, SLENDER LEGS.

TAIL
LONG AND TAPERING AND FREE FROM ANY DEFECT.

ABOVE
An Oriental Chocolate Spotted Tabby showing good round spots that are evenly distributed.

LEFT
Whatever the colour, the Ticked Tabby should have an evenly ticked coat with two, or preferably three, bands of colour on each hair. It is acceptable for the undersides to show slight tabby markings, but the main part of the coat should be free of spots, stripes or other markings.

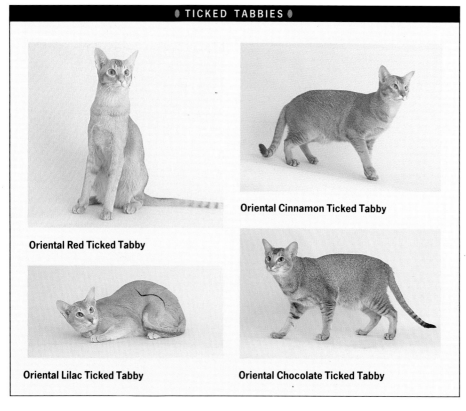

TICKED TABBIES

Oriental Red Ticked Tabby

Oriental Cinnamon Ticked Tabby

Oriental Lilac Ticked Tabby

Oriental Chocolate Ticked Tabby

Tabby

Tabbies are available with four different patterns: classic, spotted, mackerel and ticked. In total, Tabbies are available in more than thirty different colours. The coat and eye colour should be as laid down for the self colour.

Smokes, Shaded and Tipped

With these varieties the coat is not visibly patterned; each single hair has a different amount of colouring giving a uniform effect. In the Tipped there is only a small amount of colour visible at the tip of each hair; in the Smoke it is quite the reverse, with the coat colour extending almost to the skin. The Shaded is in-between these two. Again, it is possible to breed this series in all the colour variations.

ANGORA

The Angora is to the Oriental what the Balinese is to the Siamese: a longhaired variety of what is usually thought of as a shorthaired breed. The fur is neither as long nor as dense as the Persian and is easier to groom. In all other respects, including character and temperament, it is essentially Oriental. Angoras can be bred in all the variations of colour and pattern acceptable for the Orientals.

● ADVANTAGES ●

● Very elegant and attractive.
● Short, close-lying coats that neither require much grooming nor shed to any great degree.
● Intelligent, affectionate and playful temperaments.
● Companionable.

● DISADVANTAGES ●

● Very loud voices, especially when calling.
● Incessant talkers.
● Can be destructive if left alone for any period of time.
● Angoras will need additional, frequent grooming.

RIGHT
The Angora is the longhaired variety of Oriental, and has a distinctive silk-like sheen to the coat. In general type and conformation, the standards are the same as the Oriental.

OTHER SHORTHAIR BREEDS

All breeds of shorthaired cats other than British and American, Burmese, Siamese and Oriental, are classified in the UK as Foreign Shorthairs; for the purposes of this book, I am also including in this section other shorthair breeds that are available only in certain countries.

The only characteristic these breeds all have in common is their outgoing personalities, and even so some are more demanding than others; their fur colour, patterning and texture are all completely different. These cats come from all four corners of the world, and there are many varieties. Some breeds have been imported to the West from distant countries, where they have been known for centuries – the Abyssinian, for example, thought to be a descendant of the original Egyptian cats, and the elegant Korat, the 'Si-Sawat' or sacred cat of Thailand. Then there are the naturally mutated breeds, such as the furless Sphynx, and the curly-coated Rex breeds; and also the newer, man-made 'designer' breeds, genetically manufactured by breeders, such as the Burmilla, Bengal and Ocicat.

ABYSSINIAN
(and Somali)

History

This is an old cat breed and is thought to have been imported into the UK from Abyssinia, now Ethiopia. The shape, size and distinctive coat bear a considerable resemblance to the mummified cats found in Egyptian tombs, and the wall paintings that depicted Bast and other feline gods. It is possible that the Abyssinian is directly descended from the sacred cats of Ancient Egypt, which gives a certain romance to the breed.

In recent years, a longhaired variety, known as the Somali, has been recognized. It is likely that these longhaired cats have been around for many years but, in the past, were considered to be

BELOW
The Somali is basically a longhaired Abyssinian; it conforms to the standards for this breed other than the length of fur, and is available in just as many colours.

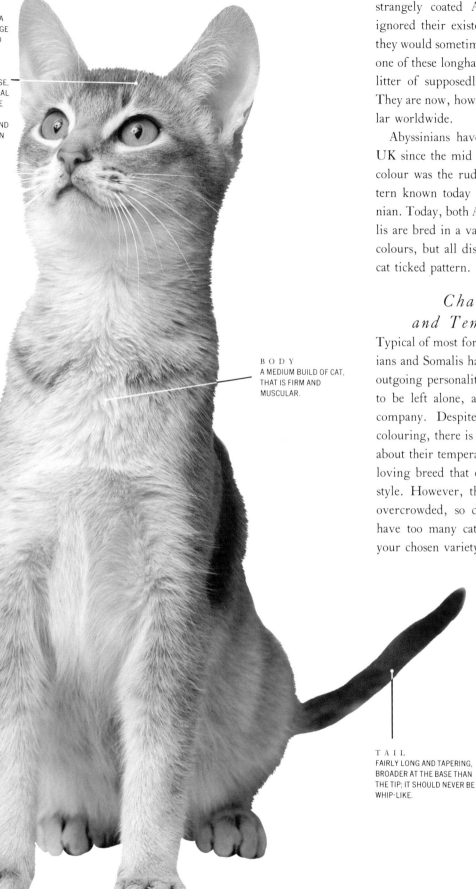

HEAD
THE HEAD SHOULD HAVE A MODERATE, MEDIUM WEDGE AND THE MUZZLE SHOULD HAVE GENTLE CONTOURS WITHOUT BEING SHARPLY POINTED. THE EARS ARE LARGE, BROAD AT THE BASE, WIDE SET AND WITH TYPICAL EAR 'TUFTS'. THE EYES ARE LARGE AND EXPRESSIVE, WITH AN ORIENTAL SET, AND SHOULD BE AMBER, GREEN OR HAZEL.

BODY
A MEDIUM BUILD OF CAT, THAT IS FIRM AND MUSCULAR.

TAIL
FAIRLY LONG AND TAPERING, BROADER AT THE BASE THAN THE TIP; IT SHOULD NEVER BE WHIP-LIKE.

strangely coated Abyssinians. Breeders ignored their existence to the point that they would sometimes not even admit that one of these longhairs had been born to a litter of supposedly 'pure' Abyssinians. They are now, however, extremely popular worldwide.

Abyssinians have been known in the UK since the mid 1800s, when the coat colour was the ruddy brown ticked pattern known today as the 'usual' Abyssinian. Today, both Abyssinians and Somalis are bred in a variety of different coat colours, but all display the typical wildcat ticked pattern.

Character and Temperament

Typical of most foreign breeds, Abyssinians and Somalis have highly intelligent, outgoing personalities. They do not like to be left alone, and will pine without company. Despite their wild-cat coat colouring, there is very little that is wild about their temperament; they are a very loving breed that enjoy a domestic lifestyle. However, they do not like to be overcrowded, so do not be tempted to have too many cats if an Abyssinian is your chosen variety.

LEFT
The Blue Abyssinian shows a pale oatmeal undercoat ticked with deep slate-blue.

RIGHT
The Usual Abyssinian
has a golden-brown
body colour, with
black ticking, and the
base fur should be
ruddy or apricot.

BELOW
The Sorrel Somali has
a coat of warm copper
ticked with chocolate.

Type and Standard of Points

This should be a medium-sized cat with a close-lying ticked coat that shows a lustrous sheen. The general appearance should be of an elegant cat: the head is a round, wedge shape; the ears large and wide-set with tufted tips; the neck long, and the legs long and slender; and the tail, tapering at the tip, in proportion to the length of the body.

The eye colour should be amber, green or hazel, and the coat is now accepted in many colours: usual, sorrel, blue, chocolate, lilac, silver, fawn, red, cream, and the associated colours of tortie.

LEFT
A Sorrel Abyssinian showing the distinctive ticked coat pattern.

AMERICAN WIREHAIR AND AMERICAN CURL

History

Both these breeds are domestic short-hair varieties that display the effect of a naturally mutated gene which has only been seen in the USA to date. The American Curl has ears that curl away from the face; a misshapen ear is also seen in the Scottish Fold, but with that breed the ear flops forwards.

The American Wirehair has a unique wiry coat that is not dissimilar to that of the Cornish and Devon Rex varieties. However, the genes causing the ear shape and coat texture are quite different to those responsible for the Scottish Fold and the Rexes.

Character and Temperament

Both the Wirehair and Curl display the temperament and character associated with the other American Shorthair varieties (*see 'British and American Shorthairs'*). They are friendly, intelligent, sturdy and adaptable and make excellent pets.

Type and Standard of Points

In general, both are medium-sized breeds, with rounded heads, medium-sized, wide-set ears, and with well-developed muzzles and distinctive whisker pads. They are not as cobby or short-faced as the American or British Shorthair, and in general tend to be more elegant and graceful, similar to the general build of the Foreign Shorthairs.

ASIAN CATS
(*including Burmilla*)

History

This breed was the result of a modern-day Romeo and Juliet story. It was created by accident, when two lovers were barred from seeing each other. A Chinchilla male lived in the same home as a female Lilac Burmese; as youngsters, they loved to play together but when the female began to show signs of coming in to call, she was isolated in the study until she could be taken to her pre-arranged assignment with a suitable Burmese 'husband-to-be'. Unfortunately – or fortunately perhaps for the cats and the lovers of this charming new breed – the cleaner left the study door open and allowed the lovelorn Chinchilla access to his girlfriend. The resulting kittens were so instantly attractive that the owner decided that they should be given a special name, and nicknamed them 'Burmillas'.

There was no problem in finding new homes for these little cross-bred kittens; indeed, there was more interest in them than in the pure-bred Burmese kittens, and so a repeat mating was made. This was the beginning of what is now an increasingly popular breed, and explains how it gained its name.

Character and Temperament

The Burmilla is an outgoing, friendly and sociable cat that has inherited slightly modified characteristics from both of the original parents; it is not as noisy or demanding as the Burmese but is more adventurous and inquisitive than the Chinchilla. For anyone who likes the Burmese, but could not cope with the continual demands made by it, then perhaps a Burmilla is the ideal compromise.

BELOW

*Within the Asian Group are many colours of cat, the best known being the Burmilla (**RIGHT**); his litter brother (**LEFT**) is a Smoke.*

TAIL
AN ELEGANT, MEDIUM TO LONG TAIL IS REQUIRED, OF MEDIUM THICKNESS AND CARRIED PROUD.

BODY
IN GENERAL, ASIANS, LIKE BURMESE, ARE ELEGANT CATS OF MEDIUM TYPE, AND SHOULD ALWAYS HAVE A WELL-MUSCLED APPEARANCE.

HEAD
THE GENERAL STANDARD FOR THIS BREED IS FOR A CAT OF BURMESE TYPE. THE HEAD SHOULD HAVE A GOOD WIDTH BETWEEN THE EARS, AND, IN PROFILE, THE NOSE SHOULD SHOW A DISTINCT BREAK. THE EARS MAY HAVE SLIGHT EAR TUFTS IN THE SHORTHAIRED VARIETIES, WITH LONGER TUFTS IN THE TIFFANIE. FULL, EXPRESSIVE EYES SHOULD BE SET WIDE APART.

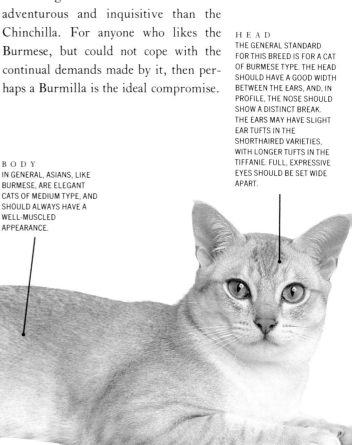

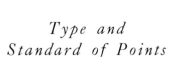

Type and Standard of Points

A breeding plan was developed to perpetuate the breed; it was decided that the Burmilla should, ideally, be a shorthaired cat of Burmese type but displaying certain traits from the Chinchilla: these included the tipped coat pattern, brick-red nose leather outlined in black, and the black markings around the eyes giving the impression that they have been outlined with mascara.

To preserve the type, the first-generation Burmillas were mated back to Burmese. This next generation gave rise to several different types of Burmilla-related cat, and at this point it was decided to use the term Asian Group to apply to all the genetic possibilities associated with this breed. This includes not just Burmillas which may be shaded or tipped, but also the self shorthair – known as a Bombay if it is Black, and an Asian if it is any other colour – the longhair version, or Tiffanie, and four varieties of Asian Tabby – Spotted, Classic, Mackerel and Ticked.

In the USA, the term Bombay refers to a Black Burmese that has resulted from a cross between a Burmese and a Black American Shorthair; the Tiffany (spelt with a 'y' not 'ie') was the result of an original cross between a Burmese and a Self Longhair.

RIGHT
One of the original four Burmillas, the result of a mating between a love-lorn Chinchilla male and the object of his desires, a Lilac Burmese female. This was the start of a whole new group of cats.

BELOW
The Tiffanie (Tiffany in the USA) is the longhaired variety of the Asian (longhaired version of the Burmese in the USA).

BELOW
The Asian Ticked Tabby showing the distinctive 'M' marking on the forehead.

BENGAL

(and Leopard Cat)

History

The spotted cat has always been highly popular, probably because the markings remind us of true wild cats. The idea of a small spotted leopard cat with the temperament of the domestic moggie seemed appealing, and so it was decided to try to breed such a cat.

In America in the early 1960s, the first planned mating took place between a domestic shorthaired cat and an Asian leopard cat, but it was not until the late 1980s that a structured breeding plan was developed. This was the beginning of the breed that we now call the Bengal. An American geneticist was particularly interested in these cross-matings, as it appeared that the Asian leopard cats did not have the feline leukaemia genome in their DNA structure, and so were immune to this virus. This made the Bengal a very sturdy breed.

As their popularity increased, they were seen on exhibition at cat shows and by 1991 were granted championship status by The Independent Cat Association (TICA) in the USA. More recently, they have been imported into the UK, where a new breeding plan has been set up.

Character and Temperament

Although a comparatively large breed, it is friendly, loving, alert, curious and intelligent. The Bengal has little fear of other cats, or any other animal, and makes a charming pet.

Type and Standard of Points

The general appearance should be of a large cat, with a coat pattern and colour mimicking that of the wild leopard cat; of equal importance is the temperament, which should be gentle and friendly. The cat should be sleek and very muscular, with the hind quarters slightly taller than the front. The coat, which should be spotted and show a distinct contrast between the spots and background colour, has an unusual texture which is more like a wild-cat's pelt than a domestic cat's fur. The head is a modified, broad, long wedge, with distinctive whisker pads, and the ears are short, medium-set and with a broad base ending in rounded tips.

BOMBAY

(see Asian Cats, including Burmilla)

BURMILLA

(see Asian Cats, including Burmilla)

LEFT
The Bengal, although popular in the USA for many years, has only recently arrived in the UK.

BELOW
The Snow Leopard Cat is the silver version of the Bengal.

EXOTIC SHORTHAIR
(see Longhairs, Persian Type)

MANX
(see British Shorthairs)

EGYPTIAN MAU

History

T he name Mau comes from the Egyptian word for cat, and the breed is basically a spotted variety of modified Siamese type. Although the GCCF in the UK used this title for many years, the breed is now referred to as the Oriental Spotted Tabby. In the USA it is still known as the Egyptian Mau where, over the years, it has developed a type quite distinct from that of the Siamese and Orientals.

Despite their glamorous name, Egyptian Maus do not come from Egypt, but have been bred for a coat pattern that resembles that of the cats in Ancient Egypt. The breed was first developed in Europe in the mid 1950s and, later that decade, was exported to the USA where it has remained popular.

Character and Temperament

As with any breed that has Siamese or Oriental ancestry, this is an outgoing, adventurous, intelligent and friendly cat that loves company and does not like to be left alone. One word of warning: as their coat pattern is so distinctive, these cats are more likely to be stolen than many other varieties and should be carefully watched if they are to be allowed outside.

Type and Standard of Points

The Mau should generally be of a modified Siamese type. The head should show a rounded wedge and, in profile, should not be as straight as the Siamese or Oriental varieties. The tail should be of medium length, tapering at the tip – not a Siamese 'whip' tail, as this is considered a fault. The eyes should be almond-shaped, neither too Oriental nor too round, and pale green. The coat is accepted in five colours: black, smoke, pewter, bronze and silver.

ABOVE
The Egyptian Mau is an American breed not dissimilar to the Oriental Spotted Tabby seen in the UK, but with less extreme Oriental type.

Character and Temperament

This is a most friendly breed and makes a perfect pet. It has a sweet disposition and is intelligent. It gets on very well with most other animals, and loves human company.

Type and Standard of Points

This is a medium-sized slender cat but has a feel of muscularity despite its dainty appearance. Typically, the hind legs, like on the Manx, are longer than the front legs. The tail should be carried upright when the cat is relaxed and the fur should radiate to give a similar effect to that of a well-clipped poodle. The eyes are large, oval and slanting and the head should be similar in shape to that of the Siamese, an equilateral triangle from ears to nose. Traditionally black, white and red, or tortie-and-white, many other colours and patterns are likewise accepted.

ABOVE

The Japanese Bobtail, or 'Mi-Ke' cat, originates from Japan and is a popular breed in America; it is not available in the UK.

KORAT

History

The Korat is one of the oldest breeds, originating from Thailand where it was known as the sacred cat, 'Si-Sawat'. It first came to America in the early 1950s and from there arrived in the UK in 1972. The Thai name for the breed means good fortune and in their own country Korats have always been highly prized. They are a unique breed as they are only available in the original blue colour.

JAPANESE BOBTAIL

History

Not a completely tail-less variety, as some Manx, this cat shows a short 'bobbed' tail. It originates from Japan, where it is known as the 'Mi-Ke' and is considered a symbol of friendship and hospitality. The Japanese often have ceramic cats of Mi-Ke type, with one paw in the air, displayed in their homes as a symbol of welcome.

Character and Temperament

This is a quiet, gentle, loving breed with the sweetest of temperaments. It may seem placid, but is intelligent. It does not like loud noises or an unruly household so is best suited to a quiet home.

Type and Standard of Points

The most striking feature of the Korat is its sweet, heart-shaped face with lustrous round green-to-yellow eyes; the Korat's expression is quite distinctive. The head should show a gently pointed muzzle and the ears should be of medium size and set high on the head. In profile the nose should show a slight break. The coat should be short, sleek and close-lying, displaying an even silvery-blue colour all over, and, in profile, breaks in the fur along the backbone. In general, the Korat should be a medium-sized cat that is muscular and firm.

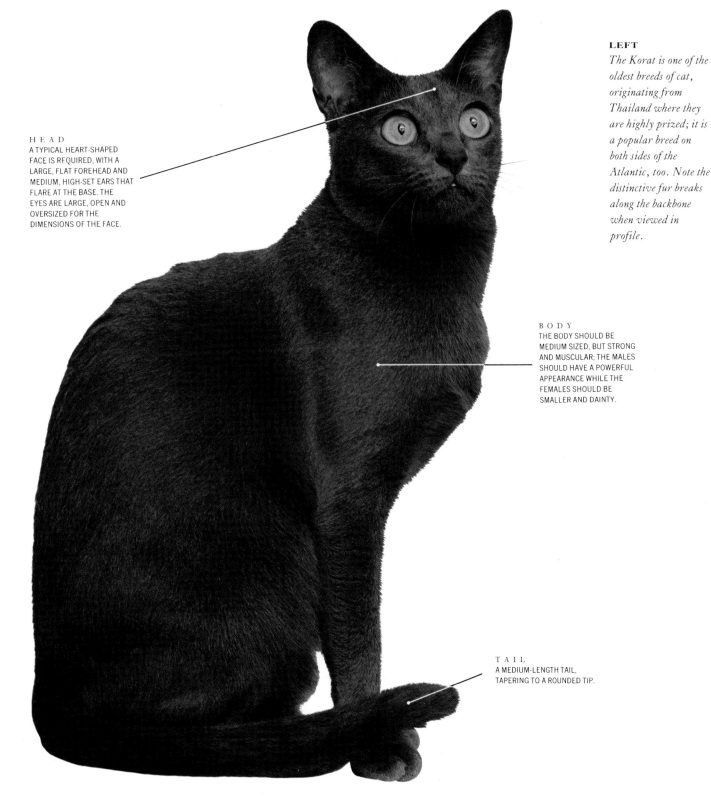

HEAD
A TYPICAL HEART-SHAPED FACE IS REQUIRED, WITH A LARGE, FLAT FOREHEAD AND MEDIUM, HIGH-SET EARS THAT FLARE AT THE BASE. THE EYES ARE LARGE, OPEN AND OVERSIZED FOR THE DIMENSIONS OF THE FACE.

LEFT
The Korat is one of the oldest breeds of cat, originating from Thailand where they are highly prized; it is a popular breed on both sides of the Atlantic, too. Note the distinctive fur breaks along the backbone when viewed in profile.

BODY
THE BODY SHOULD BE MEDIUM SIZED, BUT STRONG AND MUSCULAR; THE MALES SHOULD HAVE A POWERFUL APPEARANCE WHILE THE FEMALES SHOULD BE SMALLER AND DAINTY.

TAIL
A MEDIUM-LENGTH TAIL, TAPERING TO A ROUNDED TIP.

OCICAT

History

The Ocicat is another of the 'manufactured' breeds of spotted cat and is amongst the most popular; because they look rather like little ocelots, they were called 'Ocicats'.

Back in the early 1960s an American breeder was trying to develop Siamese with Abyssinian points, and so crossed a Siamese with an Abyssinian. These early litters indeed produced the pattern of Siamese desired, but they also contained assorted patterns of tabbies, including one spotted kitten who was called 'Tonga'; this little cat is generally recognized as being the first Ocicat, although he arrived as a side effect of another breeding programme.

Tonga was shown only once, in 1965, but by the end of that decade the breed had become increasingly popular and more and more Ocicats were being shown. Championship status was granted in America in 1987 by the Cat Fanciers Association (CFA), and they have recently been imported into the UK.

Character and Temperament

This is another breed that has been genetically manufactured to produce what looks like a wild cat in colour and pattern of coat. In temperament and disposition, however, it is just like any other domestic cat, and is characteristically intelligent and playful – as are all the breeds mentioned in this section.

Type and Standard of Points

The Ocicat is a moderate-type cat which should be large and well spotted. The head is a modified wedge with a broad muzzle, with just a suggestion of squareness to the jaw. In profile there should not be a visible nose break but more a gentle rise from the bridge of the nose to the brow; the chin should be strong and the jaw firm without any sign of either being overshot or undershot. The ears are quite large and set wide apart and should never be too high or too low; ear tufts are preferable but not essential and, if present, should extend vertically from the tips of the ears. The eyes should be large

ABOVE
The typical 'wild cat' expression belies the gentle, affectionate nature of the Ocicat.

and almond-shaped, displaying a good depth of colour; blue is an unacceptable colour.

The Ocicat can be bred in ten main colours, or any of these ticked with silver. In general the cat should give the appearance of elegance but muscularity and, when held, should feel heavier than its looks suggest.

REX

History

Both the Devon and Cornish are naturally mutated breeds that first appeared in the UK in the late 1950s and early 1960s. Although they both display a curly coat, genetically they are quite different. The Cornish Rex first appeared in a litter of kittens born on a farm in Cornwall; the farmer consulted his vet about one kitten that was born with this curious coat and decided to mate it back to its mother to see what the result would be; the kittens appeared with the same strange coats. A decade later, a similar curly-coated cat was seen in Devon; this was the first Devon Rex. When two Devons were mated together they did not initially produce curly-coated offspring and from this it was realized that they were a quite distinct breed from the Cornish. The Cornish were much larger, and resembled a farm cat that had been given a permanent; the Devons were

much smaller in build with large, round eyes and ears that appeared to be quite out of proportion to the size of their bodies – if they had been discovered in the 1980s, they would probably have been nick-named 'Gremlins'.

Character and Temperament

Both Rexes are a lively, intelligent and active breed. They love people and their families and adore to be included in any household activity. They can be extremely naughty – these are breeds with a pro-

BELOW
A litter of Blue-Tortie and Red Cornish Rex kittens showing the distinct curly coat.

BELOW
An adult Blue-Tortie Cornish Rex; any coat colour is acceptable for this breed.

HEAD
A MEDIUM WEDGE TAPERING TO SHOW A STRONG CHIN; THE FOREHEAD SHOULD BE FLAT, AND IN PROFILE THE NOSE SHOULD BE STRAIGHT. EARS ARE LARGE AND SET HIGH ON THE HEAD. EYES SHOULD BE MEDIUM SIZED AND OVAL IN SHAPE.

BODY
THE BODY SHOULD BE MEDIUM SIZED, SLENDER, FIRM AND MUSCULAR. THE CURLY COAT SHOULD BE SHORT AND PLUSHY, WITHOUT GUARD HAIRS, AND DISPLAY A DISTINCTIVE RIPPLED EFFECT.

TAIL
SHOULD BE LONG AND TAPERING, WITH A GOOD COVERING OF CURLY FUR.

ABOVE
A Brown-Tortie Cornish Rex showing a well-rexed coat.

RIGHT
A Cornish Si-Rex, such as this Red-point, has the restricted coat pattern of the Siamese but with a rexed coat; they are available in just as many colours as the Siamese.

found sense of humour, and they are the sort of cats that you either love or hate. The Devons sometimes have less fur but neither variety has an undercoat – this means that the Rex breeds are especially suitable for people who suffer from allergies such as asthma, as there is little fur to shed.

● REX CHARACTERISTICS ●

The Tabby Cornish Rex shows paler shading on the neck, tummy and inside legs.

The main body fur should curl, giving a wave-like, rippled effect.

Even the whiskers are crinkled, which is a point required in the standards.

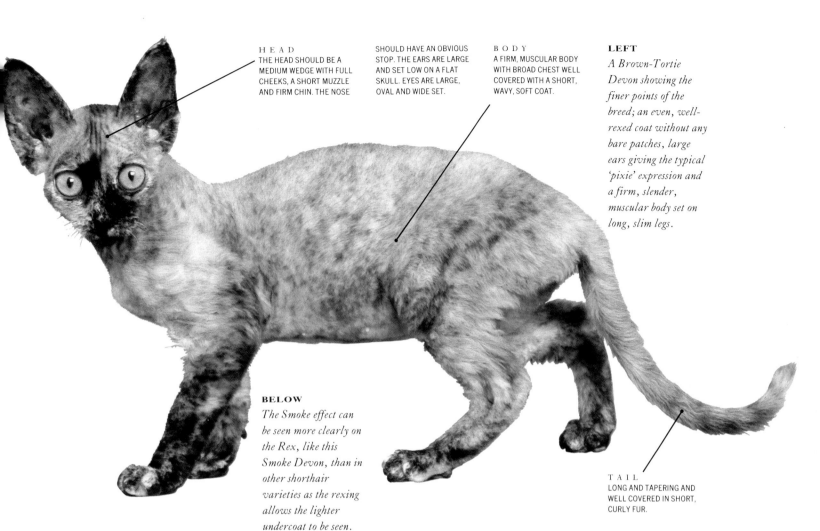

HEAD
THE HEAD SHOULD BE A
MEDIUM WEDGE WITH FULL
CHEEKS, A SHORT MUZZLE
AND FIRM CHIN. THE NOSE

SHOULD HAVE AN OBVIOUS
STOP. THE EARS ARE LARGE
AND SET LOW ON A FLAT
SKULL. EYES ARE LARGE,
OVAL AND WIDE SET.

BODY
A FIRM, MUSCULAR BODY
WITH BROAD CHEST WELL
COVERED WITH A SHORT,
WAVY, SOFT COAT.

LEFT
*A Brown-Tortie
Devon showing the
finer points of the
breed; an even, well-
rexed coat without any
bare patches, large
ears giving the typical
'pixie' expression and
a firm, slender,
muscular body set on
long, slim legs.*

BELOW
*The Smoke effect can
be seen more clearly on
the Rex, like this
Smoke Devon, than in
other shorthair
varieties as the rexing
allows the lighter
undercoat to be seen.*

TAIL
LONG AND TAPERING AND
WELL COVERED IN SHORT,
CURLY FUR.

Type and Standard of Points

The Cornish should be long and elegant, but feel firm and muscular. The legs should be long, the head wedge-shaped and in profile showing a long straight nose. The eyes should be oval and the ears large and set wide apart, in a similar way to the Siamese but not so extreme. The coat should cover the body well but show distinct rexing. The Devon is altogether much smaller and does not have such profuse fur as the Cornish: it is an unusual-looking cat and not to every-body's taste. The head is round, showing a definite nose break in profile, and with distinctive large ears. As the coat is shorter than the Cornish, there are times when it can look somewhat bald. Both Devons and Cornish are available in any colour, pattern or combination of both.

RUSSIAN BLUE

History

This is another all-blue variety, but the coat colour and texture is quite different from that seen in other blue cats such as the British, Burmese and Korat. It is a cat thought to have originated from Archangel (Archangel'sk) in Russia, hence its other name, Archangel cat. Cats with similar coat colour are to be found in northern Scandinavia, so it is possible that the breed did originate in Russia and travelled to Europe by way of sailors and their ships.

Character and Temperament

Quiet, shy, loving and gentle is probably the best way to sum up the breed. Russians do not like noisy households as they are somewhat thoughtful and pensive – if they liked music, they would prefer Mozart to Wagner. They become very attached to their owners, and are quite content to be confined indoors as long as they have the company of their preferred human.

Type and Standard of Points

Russians should be medium to large-sized shorthair cats that exude elegance. They are most graceful and have been likened to ballerinas, as they appear to be walking on 'points' when they move. The fur is unusual as it is a short plush, with a typically double coat; this probably derived from the cat's need for warmth in the cold Russian winters. More recently, White Russians have appeared, but this has not been considered a worthwhile breeding programme to follow.

HEAD
THE HEAD IS A SHORT WEDGE WITH DISTINCT WHISKER PADS. THE EARS ARE LARGE AND POINTED, SET UPRIGHT; THE HEAD SHOULD BE FLAT BETWEEN THE EARS. THE EYES ARE ALMOND SHAPED AND WIDE SET.

RIGHT
The Russian Blue is an elegant cat with long, slender limbs. Although white and black Russians have been seen, there has been little interest in furthering these newer colours and the blue remains the classic example of this breed.

BODY
THE BODY IS LONG AND GRACEFUL WITH LONG LEGS; THE COAT IS QUITE DISTINCT AND SHOULD BE DOUBLE, THICK, SHORT AND SILKY.

TAIL
LONG AND TAPERING BUT IN PROPORTION TO THE BODY.

SCOTTISH FOLD

History

Although not recognized in the UK, because the deformed ears are considered an unacceptable defect detrimental to the cat's health, the breed is recognized in the USA where it is quite popular. Like the Rex varieties, the breed developed from a natural mutation and, as the name suggests, was first seen in Scotland.

Character and Temperament

Although they have a somewhat strange appearance, the Scottish Fold is a sweet, gentle breed. They are good with children, other cats and pets, and although the shape of the ear may make you suspect that these cats have problems with hearing, this has never been known to be the case.

Type and Standard of Points

In shape the cat should be of moderated British type but always showing the distinctive ears, which are folded forwards and downwards. The coat should be thick and resilient, similar to that of the Manx and other shorthair breeds that have come from the cold north. The ears should be set wide apart so that the head has a completely flat appearance. Both coat and eye colour can be of any hue.

SINGAPURA

History

This breed gained its name from Singapore where it was considered to be the 'drain' cat that lived in the gutters – which is the accepted explanation for it being smaller than most other foreign shorthairs. As Singapore is a colony containing many cat-loving 'expats', these diminutive, indigenous cats were im-

mediately taken to their hearts. The slight size of the Singapura may be attributed to its deprived background, but it is generally a sturdy breed.

Character and Temperament

What it lacks in size it makes up for in character and temperament. Singapuras are sweet, loving and affectionate, although perhaps a little demure and reserved.

Type and Standard of Points

The general appearance is of a small cat that feels heavier than it looks. The ticked tabby coat looks similar to that of the Abyssinian. The ears should be large, slightly pointed and wide at the base; the eyes are large and almond-shaped and the head should be rounded, narrowing to a blunt muzzle and in profile showing a slight nose break and a firm chin and jaw line.

ABOVE
The Scottish Fold, although originating in the UK, is now almost unknown this side of the Atlantic, while it is a popular breed in America.

LEFT
The Singapura, available in Europe and America but only recently imported into the UK, originates from Singapore.

SNOWSHOE

History

S ometimes referred to as a Short-haired Birman, the Snowshoe bears no ancestry from this ancient and original breed of cat. It is, in fact, the result of mating a Siamese with an American Bi-colour Shorthair, which provided the gene necessary for the typical white pattern on the feet.

Character and Temperament

These are sweet-natured cats, displaying a modified form of the Siamese intelligence crossed with the laid-back nature of the American Shorthair – possibly the perfect combination for a pet.

Type and Standard of Points

This is quite a large breed with a short close-lying coat which may be of any colour acceptable for the Siamese or any other breed with the Himalayan factor. The eyes should always be blue, large and almond-shaped. The head should be a medium triangular wedge, in profile showing a definite nose break, but never being of Siamese type which is considered a severe fault. The muzzle and feet must be characteristically white.

SPHYNX

History

T his breed is a natural mutation, first seen in Canada in 1966. Although there have been reports of hairless cats in other parts of the world, this is the only one to have been bred from, with the idea of establishing a breeding programme to perpetuate the line.

Character and Temperament

Sphynx display an outgoing character not dissimilar to that of the Rex – if you do not have much fur you have to have something going for you. This breed is certainly a conversation piece and it does not appear to suffer much from the cold, although additional heating is probably most appreciated.

Type and Standard of Points

The most important point for the Sphynx is a complete lack of fur; it is a fault for even a slight down to be perceptible. Most important is the colour, pigmentation and pattern of the skin. The body should feel hard and muscular with long, slim legs, slender neck, and long tapering tail. The head should be longer than it is wide, with a smooth profile and distinctive whisker pads.

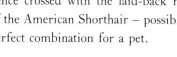

*The Tonkinese is a cross between Burmese and Siamese and is available in many colours including Blue (**RIGHT**), Lilac (**ABOVE**) and Chocolate (**BELOW**).*

TONKINESE

History

Tonkinese are basically a cross between Burmese and Siamese. They, therefore, display a little of each of these well-known breeds. They arrived by way of a breeding programme developed in North America in the late 1960s and early 1970s. Although accepted there in 1975, they are still only granted provisional status in the UK and Europe.

Character and Temperament

As with Burmese and Siamese, the Tonkinese is an outgoing, friendly and affectionate cat that will be into anything and everything.

Type and Standard of Points

In shape and size, the Tonkinese is a modified form of its original parentage; neither as long and angular as the Siamese nor as chunky as the Burmese, but a true cross between the two. Recently this breed has been given provisional status in the UK by the GCCF.

BURMESE

Although Burmese are relative newcomers to the cat fancy, they are probably one of the most popular breeds in the world today. Brown cats are reported to have existed in the Far East, particularly Thailand and Burma, hundreds of years ago; as with many travellers' tales, fact and fiction tend to get a bit muddled up. Burmese are said to have been the original 'guard cats' for the Burmese temples – but the Birman breed also lays claim to this fame too.

◆ HISTORY ◆

The first 'Burmese' seen in the West was a small, brown female called Wong Mau, brought into America from the Far East in 1930. At this point, there was no similar male cat to mate her to and so it was decided that her beau should be a male of the breed with the closest resemblance to herself, a Seal-point Siamese. Her kittens from this litter were hybrids, close to what we now call the Tonkinese. Genetically, it is most likely that Wong Mau herself was a dark variation of a Tonkinese as when one of her sons was mated back to her, the progeny included dark brown cats like herself. These are generally regarded as the first real Burmese cats.

It was not until 1948 that Burmese found their way across the Atlantic to Britain. Burmese are not as instantly appealing, glamorous and recognizably pedigree as the Siamese; however, their intelligence and character combined with a marvellous temperament soon won them popularity. They also have the added advantage that their voices are not quite as loud as the Siamese.

As their popularity increased, and more kittens were bred, a great surprise occurred. In 1955, a silvery grey kitten appeared in a litter. It was the first Blue Burmese and was quite aptly named Sealcoat Blue Surprise. This proved that Burmese had a similar genetic make-up to Siamese: Brown Burmese is genetically equivalent to Seal-point Siamese; Blue Burmese equivalent to Blue-point Siamese. This was just the beginning. In America, a dilute version of the Brown Burmese had been noted, which was called Champagne, and a much paler version of the Blue, which was termed Platinum. These colours correspond to the Chocolate- and Lilac-point Siamese, and in the UK they are known as Chocolate and Lilac Burmese.

Once the basic genetics of the Burmese cat were understood, a whole spectrum of colour possibilities could be created. If breeders had managed to introduce the sex-linked colours to Siamese (red, cream and tortie) then why not try to produce Burmese in these colours too? A sensible breeding plan was inaugurated by several breeders, and with the help of the Burmese Cat Club in the UK to implement this programme, we now have Burmese cats in ten different colours – all of which have the health, stamina, type and temperament of the original 'Little Brown Cat', as Wong Mau was affectionately called – the little brown cat that came to the USA sixty years ago.

Burmese can now be seen in the following colours, although their titles differ in the UK and the USA: Brown (USA, Sable); Blue; Chocolate (USA, Champagne); Lilac (USA, Platinum); Red; Cream; Brown-Tortie; Blue-Tortie; Chocolate-Tortie; Lilac-Tortie. In some American cat fancies, Burmese other than Brown, Chocolate and Lilac are known as Malayans; in other fancies, the sex-linked colours are not recognized at all.

Character and Temperament

This is a quite enchanting breed, but possibly not one for the faint-hearted. The Burmese have very out-going personalities and in the past have been called the 'dog cat' due to their ability to retrieve and their loyalty to their owners. Their voices are quieter than the Siamese, but in many respects their character is similar. Burmese do not like being left alone for long without companionship, but this does not always have to be of the human variety. Another cat, or even a dog, will provide entertainment during the day if you are out at work. There is no denying that Burmese are a demanding breed – they will not tolerate being left out of the household hubbub, and they do like to be thought of as part of the family.

ABOVE

A stunning example of a Chocolate Burmese, showing the correct golden chartreuse eye colour, and an even, warm chocolate coat colour.

Type and Standard of Points

For any Burmese, the type and body shape should be the same. Burmese are a medium-sized, sturdy and well-muscled breed; they should never be as large and heavily boned as the British, nor as long and slender as the Siamese. The head should have a well-rounded dome, both in profile and front-on, with wide-set ears of medium size. The nose should show a distinct 'break', and the chin should be strong and firm. The eyes should be an almond shape and the colour, for perfection, should be any hue of chartreuse yellow, although in the UK a pale green-yellow is acceptable in an otherwise out-standing specimen. A typical Burmese conforming to these standards will have what is called the typical 'wicked' Burmese look.

The tail should be in proportion to the body length – a simple guide is that the tail should just reach the shoulder blade of the cat. It should have no visible kink or fault.

The coat should be short, close-lying, and of a clear colour. In Chocolate and Lilac Burmese it is acceptable for the points to be slightly darker, but it is preferable if the coat is of a uniform hue. In kittens, slight barring on the legs is permissible but in an adult cat this is considered a serious fault.

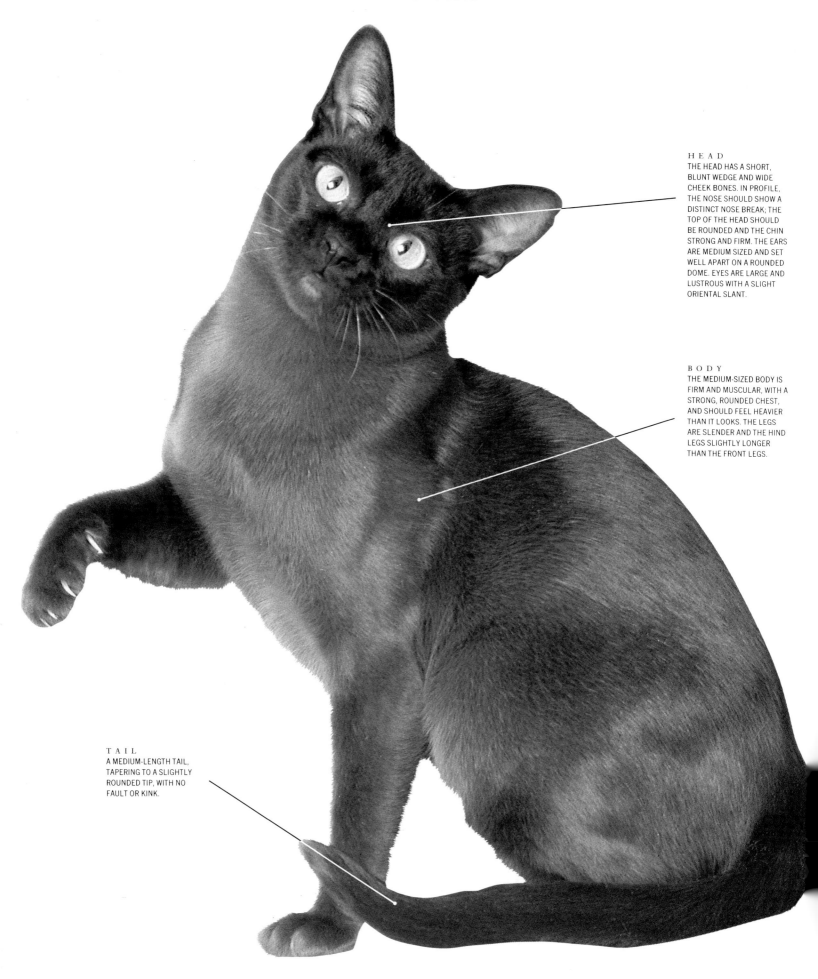

HEAD
THE HEAD HAS A SHORT, BLUNT WEDGE AND WIDE CHEEK BONES. IN PROFILE, THE NOSE SHOULD SHOW A DISTINCT NOSE BREAK; THE TOP OF THE HEAD SHOULD BE ROUNDED AND THE CHIN STRONG AND FIRM. THE EARS ARE MEDIUM SIZED AND SET WELL APART ON A ROUNDED DOME. EYES ARE LARGE AND LUSTROUS WITH A SLIGHT ORIENTAL SLANT.

BODY
THE MEDIUM-SIZED BODY IS FIRM AND MUSCULAR, WITH A STRONG, ROUNDED CHEST, AND SHOULD FEEL HEAVIER THAN IT LOOKS. THE LEGS ARE SLENDER AND THE HIND LEGS SLIGHTLY LONGER THAN THE FRONT LEGS.

TAIL
A MEDIUM-LENGTH TAIL, TAPERING TO A SLIGHTLY ROUNDED TIP, WITH NO FAULT OR KINK.

Coat Colours

Brown
(USA, SABLE)

Brown Burmese should show a deep, even, warm brown colour with no visible bars or stripes on an adult; faint 'ghost' markings are permissible on a kitten. The coat may shade to a slightly lighter tone on the underparts. The nose leather and paw pads should be dark brown.

Blue

A soft, silvery grey is the best way to describe the colour of a Blue Burmese, again allowing for a slight variation of shading to a lighter hue on the under-parts. The paw pads and nose leather should be grey.

Chocolate
(USA, CHAMPAGNE)

Warm, milk chocolate is the colour that is called for, although the face, legs and tail can be slightly darker, but never as dark as a Brown Burmese. The nose leather and paw pads should be of a chocolate-brown colour.

OPPOSITE

The Brown Burmese is the oldest of the ten colours available, and still one of the most popular; the coat on this cat is typical for the breed and colour, and shows the correct glossy sheen.

BELOW

The required standards for Burmese differ in the USA to the UK. The American-type Burmese, as seen in this Brown, requires for a much shorter face, with rounder eyes and a generally cobbier appearance than the English counterpart.

ABOVE

A Blue Burmese youngster showing the correct soft silver-grey coat colour and silver sheen around the face and ears.

Lilac
(USA, PLATINUM)

Lilac Burmese have a most attractive colouring which should be a pale dove-grey, with a slight pinkish tinge for perfection. Like the other dilute colour, chocolate, it is acceptable for the extremities to be slightly darker. Nose leather and paw pads should be lavender-pink.

Red

'Tangerine' is the best description of the Red Burmese; however, the colour should not be too hot and certainly not so cool as to be confused with a Cream Burmese. The nose leather and paw pads should be pink.

RIGHT
An adult Red Burmese showing the correct tangerine colour.

BELOW
*The coat colour is paler in kittens and young adults, as seen in this pair of Red (**LEFT**) and Chocolate (**RIGHT**) brothers.*

RIGHT

This adult male Lilac Burmese shows the correct pinky tinge to the lilac coat and the 'jowled' look typical of the entire male.

LEFT
The Cream Burmese should be a rich cream colour, with a distinct 'powdering' effect around the face, ears and legs as if the cat has been lightly dusted with talcum powder.

Cream

Cream Burmese have a pale, clotted-cream colour, with a distinctive 'powdering' over their ears and heads – looking as if they have had a light sprinkling of talcum powder. Like Red Burmese their nose leather and paw pads should be a pale pink.

Brown-Tortie

For this colour a combination of brown, red and cream colours, all intermingled, is required, with the paw pads and nose leather a combination of brown or pink, or both.

Blue-Tortie

Previously called the Blue-Cream, which exactly describes the colour required: a combination of blue and cream. Paw pads and nose leather should be the same, a mixture of blue and cream.

BELOW
The Blue-Tortie Burmese, showing the correct coat – a mixture of blue and cream.

ABOVE
Tortoiseshell Burmese, such as this Brown-Tortie, are one of the most recent colours; they arrived by way of the breeding programme designed to produce Red and Cream Burmese by British breeders during the mid 1960s.

Chocolate-Tortie

The colour of the coat should be a well-mingled combination of chocolate and cream, with the nose leather and paw pads of the same colour.

Lilac-Tortie

Lilac and cream coat, with paw pads and nose leather a dove-grey.

● ADVANTAGES ●

● Very affectionate.
● Easy to groom.
● Good with children and other animals; do not object to noisy households.
● Companionable and sensitive to owners' moods and feelings.
● Playful.

● DISADVANTAGES ●

● Do not like to be left alone without a companion.
● Demanding: will want a lot of your time and attention.
● Probably the best exponents of escapology since Houdini. Keep confined if possible.
● Overtrusting so, unless trained, at risk of being stolen.

ABOVE
A Grand Champion Chocolate-Tortie Burmese showing excellent type and coat colour.

RIGHT
In profile, the Burmese head should show a distinct nose break, with a strong jaw and chin, and the top of head should show a well rounded dome; this Chocolate-Tortie sums up the standards beautifully.

RIGHT
*The Lilac-Tortie
Burmese coat contains
a mixture of lilac and
cream; notice that even
the nose leather shows
tortie markings.*

SIAMESE

The Siamese is one of the oldest breeds of pedigree cat, and over the years many stories have been told about it, for the most part romantic fables, but perhaps there is an element of truth in some of them. Certainly, they add to the charm of this most exotic, oriental and somewhat inscrutable breed.

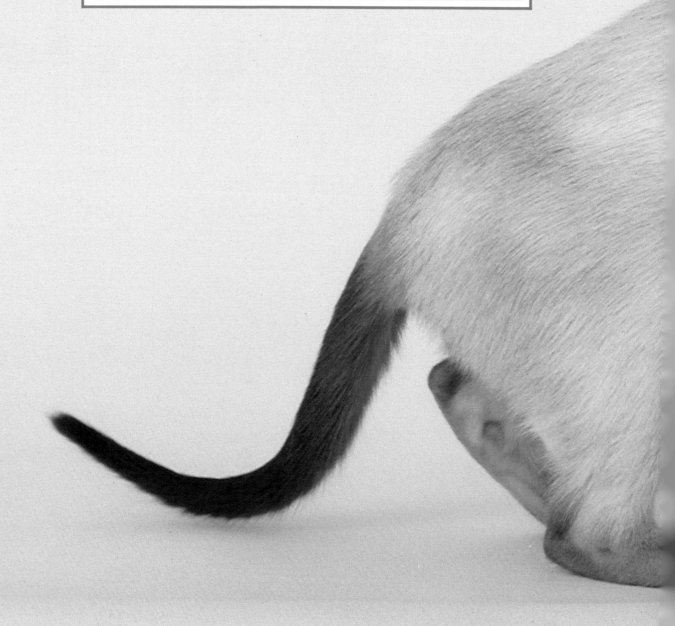

◆ HISTORY ◆

Of all the pedigree varieties, the Siamese is the most instantly recognizable. Long, lithe and elegant, with its distinctive darker 'points', it has always had great appeal.

Early Siamese tended to have eye squints and kinked tails, now regarded as serious faults, but with careful, selective breeding they have been mainly eliminated from the modern cat. Yet, these characteristics were once so prevalent that fables exist to this day 'explaining' how they were acquired.

It is said that Siamese cats were once sacred cats, guarding the Buddhist temples. One day, a valuable goblet went missing and a pair of the cats was dispatched to find the stolen treasure. After a long journey, the goblet was discovered and the female cat stayed to guard it while her male partner went back to tell the good news. So worried was she that the goblet might go missing again, that she wound her tail tightly around its stem and it became permanently kinked. For days and nights she sat watching over the prized goblet, never letting her eyes wander away, and by the time her partner returned, her eyes had developed a squint. Later she produced a litter of kittens – all of which had kinked tails and squints, because of her vigilance in guarding the lost treasure.

Another fable relates to a Siamese princess who, fearing that her rings would be stolen, entrusted her Siamese cat to guard them, placing them on its tail for safekeeping overnight. One night, the cat fell asleep, and all the rings fell off

*The Siamese is a long, slim and elegant cat of medium-sized build, although Siamese in the USA (**ABOVE**) have slightly different standards to those required in the UK (**LEFT**): the ears are larger and more uprightly set. However, they should exhibit, as these two Seal-point Siamese do, a pale coat colour, with well defined coloured 'points' whichever side of the Atlantic the Siamese comes from.*

her long slender tail and were lost forever. The princess decided to tie a knot in the tail to stop this ever happening again; and this could be another reason why Siamese have kinked tails.

Siamese kittens have always been highly prized. It was considered an honour for any foreigner to be presented with one of the Royal Cats of Siam, and it was an offence punishable by death for one of these cats to be stolen from the Royal Court, let alone be taken out of Siam. But, westwards they eventually came, and after many generations of selective breeding are now, along with Persian Longhairs and Burmese, among the most popular of pedigree varieties.

Siamese were originally a pale milky colour, with dark seal-coloured points on the paws, face, ears and tail. They have been known in this form for more than 200 years. In the late nineteenth century a Blue-point was recorded in the UK, but it is likely that this recessive colour had been around for some time before this. Perhaps it was not so highly regarded in Siam, and was 'swept under the carpet' as the rich Seal-point variety was more

highly prized. Over the years, dedicated breeders have worked hard to produce other colour variations in Siamese, but their names vary between the UK and North America. We now have, not only the Seal- and Blue-points, but Chocolate and Lilac (USA, Frost-point), as well as the Red-, Cream-, Tortie- and Tabby-points (USA, Colourpoint Shorthairs).

Character and Temperament

Siamese are typical of the Oriental group of cats and, like their near relations the Burmese, are a vocal breed with outgoing personalities. They are the kind of cat that you either adore or hate; they can be noisy and demanding and have a real need to be a part of the family. To aficionados, these are the plus points and they would not wish for the Siamese to be any other way. A Siamese does not like to be left on its own, so for anybody who is out at work all day, and only wants one cat, this is not the breed to select. If you want a cat that will give you life-long devotion, however, then the Siamese is for you.

Type and Standard of Points

Regardless of coat colour, the type of the cat should be the same, although standards do vary a little between those required in the UK by the GCCF and those of the various American cat fancies.

In general, the Siamese should be a medium-sized cat; long, slim, lithe and elegant, but with a definite muscular feel to it. Despite its fine bone structure (compared with the more heavily built British Shorthairs) it should be sturdy and feel much heavier than it appears. At the other end of the scale, it should never be obviously overweight to the point that it feels flabby, although some neuters can be prone to fat and a careful watch should be kept on their diet.

Looking at the cat face-on, the head should give the appearance of a triangle, topped by large, low-set, wide-spaced ears, tapering down to a pointed muzzle. In profile, the nose should be straight without any sign of a break or stop. The jaw should be firm without being either under- or over-shot. The eyes should be almond-shaped with the typical Oriental slant giving that inscrutable expression, and certainly without any trace of a squint. Whatever the coat colour, the eyes should always be of deepest sapphire-blue. The tail should be long, slender and tapering to a whip-like end; any kink or malformation is considered a serious fault. The tail should always be in proportion to the length of the cat – a rough guideline is that it should just reach the tip of the shoulder blade.

The quality, texture and the restrictive pattern of coat are what make the Siamese cat different from other shorthaired varieties. The coat should be short, sleek and fine-textured, with the fur lying close to the body. The coloured points should only be seen on the mask area of the face, the ears, legs and tail. It is considered a fault for the cat to be mismarked with lighter colours in these areas, especially around the eyes; these are commonly called 'spectacles'. Conversely, darker shading is frowned upon on the otherwise paler parts of the body.

The Siamese coat pattern is restricted to the cooler parts of the body and so, if a cat has had an operation such as spaying, it is quite likely that the post-operational shock will cause the coat to temporarily darken in that area. For the same reason, Siamese living in warmer climates tend to have paler coats than those living in cooler regions. The pointed areas should always show a uniform colour with no barring or stripes, except in the case of Tabby-points, where rings or stripes are required, and the Torties, which should show a well-mingled coat.

◆ COAT COLOURS ◆

Seal-point

A pale, even cream colour with obvious seal points restricted to the face, ears, legs and tail. The nose leather and paw pads should be a similar rich seal colour.

BELOW
The head of the Siamese, when viewed full-face, should resemble a triangle from the outward tips of the ears to the end of the muzzle.

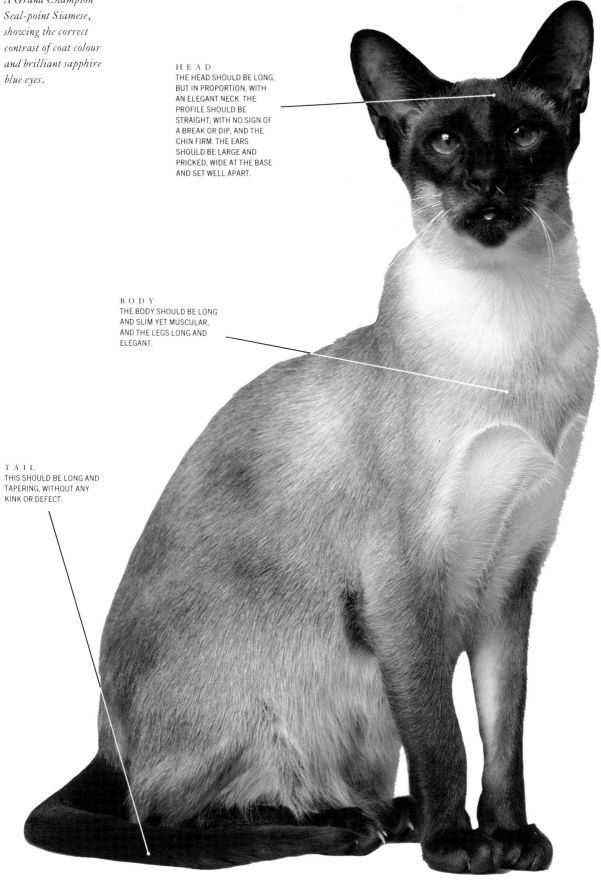

BELOW
*A Grand Champion
Seal-point Siamese,
showing the correct
contrast of coat colour
and brilliant sapphire
blue eyes.*

HEAD
THE HEAD SHOULD BE LONG,
BUT IN PROPORTION, WITH
AN ELEGANT NECK. THE
PROFILE SHOULD BE
STRAIGHT, WITH NO SIGN OF
A BREAK OR DIP, AND THE
CHIN FIRM. THE EARS
SHOULD BE LARGE AND
PRICKED, WIDE AT THE BASE
AND SET WELL APART.

BODY
THE BODY SHOULD BE LONG
AND SLIM YET MUSCULAR,
AND THE LEGS LONG AND
ELEGANT.

TAIL
THIS SHOULD BE LONG AND
TAPERING, WITHOUT ANY
KINK OR DEFECT.

ADVANTAGES

● Highly sociable (but they do expect their owners to give them their undivided attention).
● Intelligent.
● Easy to groom.
● Give almost dog-like devotion to their owners (but tend to be 'one-person' cats).

DISADVANTAGES

● Tend to have loud voices and will use them whether or not you have invited a conversation.
● Tend to be territorial and may not get on with other, less domineering breeds such as Longhairs and British Shorthairs (they usually settle well with other Orientals and Burmese).
● Because of their obvious pedigree looks, are more likely to be stolen than many breeds.

*The Siamese should always be a tall, elegant cat as well exemplified by this Blue-point (**LEFT**) and Lilac-point (**RIGHT**).*

Blue-point
Cool, glacier-white is the preferred body colour, with no sign of a creamy tinge. The points should shade to a slate-blue, with nose leather and paw pads the same.

Chocolate-point
The body should be a pale ivory colour, with points, nose leather and paw pads a pale, milky chocolate colour.

Lilac-point
(USA, FROST-POINT)
Body colour should be a glacial white, with the points showing a pale, pinkish-grey tinge. The paw pads and nose leather should be lavender-pink.

ABOVE
This Blue-point Siamese has a superb head, beautiful eye colour and the correct sheen to the coat.

BELOW
The Cream-point
Siamese has cream
points set off against a
background colour of
white shading to pale
cream on the back and
flanks.

RIGHT
The Red-point
Siamese has a white
coat, shading to pale
apricot on the back
and flanks, with
bright reddish-gold
points.

Red-point
(*USA, RED
COLOURPOINT SHORTHAIR*)

A clear white body with deep apricot-
coloured points is the ideal. Nose leather
and paw pads should be flesh-pink.

Cream-point
(*USA*, *CREAM COLOURPOINT SHORTHAIR*)

The body should be clear white, with pale, pinkish-cream points, nose leather and paw pads.

Tabby-point
(*USA*, *LYNX-POINT*),
Tortie-point and
Tortie-Tabby-point
(*USA*, *TORBIE-POINT*)

These are available in a variety of colours. The body tone should be as recommended for the solid colours, with the nose leather and paw pads similar. For the Torties the colours should be well-mingled, and the Tabby-point is the only variety of Siamese that allows for stripes on the pointed areas.

ABOVE
The Tortie-point Siamese, along with all Torties, is mostly a female-only variety; in the Siamese, the tortie markings should be restricted to the points only, as shown here.

RIGHT
This Tabby-point Supreme Grand Champion shows the correct long, elegant legs, good profile and coat, with clearly defined tabby markings on face, ears, legs and tail.

BALINESE

Balinese are, essentially, a longhaired version of the Siamese, and, in type, they should conform to the standards laid down for Siamese. Their temperament and character are slightly modified, however, probably due to the introduction of the longhair gene, so they tend to be slightly quieter and less boisterous. But the main difference is that, because they have long coats, extra grooming – and time – are required.

This longhaired variety was first seen in a litter of kittens in America. They seemed so glamorous that it was decided to breed two longhaired Siamese together to see if they bred true, which indeed they did; all the resulting kittens had long coats. The idea of a Siamese with a long, silky coat soon gained popularity, and breeders were encouraged to continue the breeding programme. By 1963, the cats were given official recognition in the USA. In the UK, things move more slowly, and it was not until the early 1980s that Balinese were granted preliminary recognition, with championship status given a few years later.

Balinese are allowed in all the colour and pattern variations that are accepted for the Siamese.

Balinese, like Siamese cats, should display their coloured points only on the mask area of the face, the ears, legs and tail as seen in this Blue Tabby-point kitten (**LEFT**) and adult stud (**BELOW**).

NON-PEDIGREE CATS

ABOVE
This well-cared-for tortie-tabby shows beautifully rich markings.

It is often said that the most beautiful cats at a cat show are to be found in the non-pedigree section, where cats of all different colours, patterns, coat lengths and type are to be seen. Many people take great pleasure in showing their rescued pets; these beautiful creatures have mostly had a deprived kittenhood and to see them exhibited in superb condition, healthy and with glossy coats, their pens festooned with ribbons and rosettes, gives their owners the credit they deserve.

Some non-pedigrees have a known ancestry; others may even have a pedigree parent or grandparent; the majority are waifs and strays, rescued by one of the charitable organizations, and have no known parentage. All deserve to be treated with the same love and care.

When choosing a non-pedigree cat or kitten, the same consideration should be given as when choosing a pedigree cat. Do not opt for a fluffy, longhaired variety if you do not have the time to spend on its grooming; a cat with a known part Siamese or Oriental background will be more likely to display the behaviour that is typical of these breeds – demanding cats with somewhat loud voices! With

LEFT
This exquisitely marked tortie-and-white is part pedigree. Her mother is a pedigree Oriental (father unknown) and she has inherited the affectionate and voluble characteristics typical of the Oriental breed.

BELOW
A typical, friendly 'moggie' with a pretty grey-and-white bi-colour coat.

RIGHT
This lovely silver tabby is hardly distinguishable from a pedigree shorthair.

BELOW
Found abandoned, dirty and mangy, the new owners had no idea of their adoptee's colour let alone his origins. Soon revealed as a red longhaired, with plenty of love and care he developed into the healthy, well-groomed and very beautiful cat seen here; he also became the Supreme Non-Pedigree.

BELOW RIGHT
These youngsters are from the same litter and show different markings. When the parentage is unknown, it can be difficult to judge the eventual size and temperament of the adult cat.

many non-pedigrees it is impossible to know what size of cat the kitten will become; at least cats do not vary in size as dogs do, so the adult cat is unlikely to outgrow your home.

● ADVANTAGES ●

● Quite often much cheaper to buy than a pedigree or may even be given free to a good home.
● Many cat shows will offer a non-pedigree section; so if you like to participate in shows you can take your moggie along.
● Available in every possible colour, pattern and fur length.
● Generally healthy, and non-fussy eaters.
● Will give you just as much love and attention as a pedigree, possibly even more.

● DISADVANTAGES ●

● If the ancestry is unknown, you will have no indication of how your kitten will develop in terms of type, temperament and size.
● An adult cat may take some time to settle into a domestic environment.
● If severely neglected, expensive veterinary bills may arise.

SHOWING YOUR CAT

The first formal show held especially for pedigree cats took place on 17 July, 1871. It was organized by Harrison Weir, the founder of the National Cat Club of the UK and took place at the Crystal Palace, in London. There were 160 exhibits at the event, all of which were judged to a specific standard, known then as the 'points of exhibition' (the predecessor of what we now call the 'standard of points'). Although the 'standards' required in the various breeds have changed dramatically over the years, the basic format of cat shows today still relies on Harrison Weir's ideas.

Originally, the National Cat Club was set up in the UK as an administrative body to govern and legislate all pedigree cats and their offspring. Today, the National is a cat club which still runs the largest cat show in the world, but the administration of pedigree cats in the UK is now the responsibility of the Governing Council of the Cat Fancy (GCCF).

As pedigree cats increased in popularity more cat clubs were founded and more shows organized. During World War II all such activities were put on hold and, although the GCCF picked up again, during this period some breeds came close to extinction. Fortunately, the dedication of cat lovers and breeders ensured that the breeding lines of these pedigree specimens were continued for present and future generations to enjoy.

In the 1990s, we have cat fancies in all four corners of the world, and many in between: North America, South Africa, Australia, New Zealand, Europe, South America and Singapore, to name a few. It seems almost every country has a space in its heart for the domestic cat, albeit a cat with an accredited parentage – the humble street cat is often forgotten.

Throughout the world, cat shows are run on the basic principle of judging the cat to a predefined standard. It is only the way in which the judging is arranged and the shows are organized that varies.

SHOWS IN THE UNITED KINGDOM

Most shows in the UK are run under the rules laid down by the GCCF. There are a few small shows organised by another group of fanciers, the Cat Association of Britain (CAB), which is affiliated to the Fédération Internationale Féline (FIFe), and these shows are run along European lines (*see 'European Shows'*). However, the majority of shows are run under the guidelines of the GCCF and their affiliated clubs. Shows take place throughout the year. Some are all-breed shows, organized by the region-

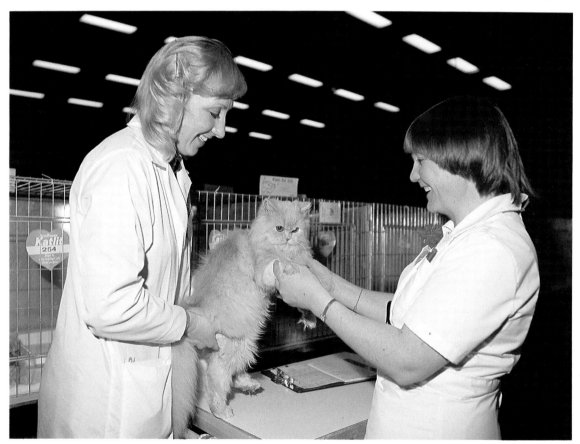

LEFT
In the UK judges go to the cats' pens to make their assessment of each exhibit; the judge is aided by a steward who pushes along the trolley, takes the cat out of the pen and generally assists the judge.

al clubs, while others are run by specific breed clubs and cater only for that particular breed. Most shows also have a non-pedigree section.

Types of Show

The GCCF licenses shows under three categories: exemption, sanction and championship.

EXEMPTION SHOWS are usually quite small affairs, often linked with a local agricultural show or similar. They are run along the lines of the GCCF, but do not have to strictly obey all the rules.

SANCTION SHOWS are like a dress rehearsal for a championship show. The classes available, the format of the show and the procedure for judging are identical to a championship show, with one exception: there are no Challenge or Premier certificates awarded, so winning exhibits cannot count any win towards the title of Champion or Premier.

There is one GCCF show that has the title of sanction, but which awards Premier certificates to the winning neuters; an anomaly it may seem, but for the simple reason that this is the annual Kensington Kitten and Neuter Cat Club Show. As there are no entire adult cats present, no Challenge certificates can be awarded, nor is it possible for a cat to be made up to Champion – so it cannot be called a championship show.

CHAMPIONSHIP SHOWS are the most popular kind as they have the bonus that the winning cats and neuters may be awarded their certificates.

Categories of Classes

There are five types of classes for pedigree exhibits: open, assessment, exhibition, miscellaneous and club (the last two commonly called the 'side' classes).

Open classes are available for all pedigree breeds, and their associated colour variations. There are separate classes for entire adults, kittens and neuter adults of each breed and colour. All adult cats have separate classes for male and female; in the case of kittens and neuters the classes may be separated by sex, depending on the number of entries. The winners of the adult and neuter classes may be awarded a Challenge certificate (entire adults) or a Premier certificate (adult neuters) if the judge feels that the overall winners are up to the prescribed standard, and are a breed with championship status. It is not unknown for such a certificate to be withheld if the exhibit is not quite up to scratch. Three such certificates, awarded by different judges, qualify the cat to use the title Champion or Premier. There are also open grand classes, which only those cats already holding the title Champion or Premier may enter; they compete within their own

group and sex (Siamese male adult, Burmese female adult, Foreign Shorthair male neuter . . .) for a coveted Grand Challenge or Grand Premier certificate. Again, three of these from three different judges qualify the cat for the title Grand Champion or Premier. All exhibits must be entered in their relevant open class, unless they are already a Champion or Premier, in which case they can opt to enter only the grand class, or both the open and the grand.

Assessment classes are for new breeds of cat to which the GCCF has awarded preliminary recognition. These are judged in the same way as the open class, but also display a provisional standard of points above their pens to help the judge assess the new breed. Those that conform to the standards will be awarded a Merit certificate.

Exhibition pens are also available at most shows and these are for cats that are not competing. Usually, exhibition pens contain cats or kittens that are of a new colour variation, or are an imported breed awaiting recognition from the GCCF. Other pens may house some famous prizewinner that the owner has decided not to put in competition any more, but which is still of great interest to fanciers. These exhibition pens are the only ones that may be decorated, and may state the name of the cats within.

The side classes are really an opportunity to get an assessment of your cats from several different judges, not just the one designated to your open class. There are various categories, such as debutante (for exhibits who have never been shown before) and limit (exhibits that have won no more than four first prizes). Your cat will also have the opportunity to compete with other types and colours of cats within its own category.

Non-pedigree exhibits have their own special section, the open classes, usually arranged by way of coat length and colour but with a special class for half-pedigree

LEFT
At GCCF shows in the UK the only decorated pens allowed are for cats that are on exhibition, and not competing; the only exception to this is the annual Supreme show where all pens are decorated.

cats. The side classes are usually more of the fun variety: classes for the cat with the largest eyes, or most expressive face – even for the one 'the judge would most like to take home'!

How to Enter a Show

The GCCF publish a list at the beginning of the show season listing all the clubs' shows, their dates, venues, the type of each show and the name and address of the show managers. Most clubs also advertise in specialist cat magazines, advising exhibitors of the date that schedules will be available and also of the closing date for entries. It is important to send off for your schedule and return the completed entry form as soon as possible; many shows have restricted space for exhibits and entries are treated on a 'first come first served' basis, with schedules being sent to club members first.

When you receive the schedule, first read through the rules carefully. Incorrect information on the entry form may disqualify your cat and any prizes won may be forfeited. Copy the name of the cat, its parents, and the registration number from your registration or transfer document. Remember that you may only show a cat if it is registered in your name.

The schedules are usually available two to three months before the show, so bear in mind that if your kitten is more than nine months old on the date of the show, it must be entered in the adult class. You may not be thinking of breeding from your cat, so it might even be a neuter by this time.

Look through the schedule, and find the open class appropriate for your breed and sex of cat; it is a common mistake to enter a neuter in the adult class, or a kitten in the neuter class. If you are in any doubt, contact your cat's breeder who should be able to advise you. Unless you are really desperate, try not to ring the show manager; he or she will be very busy sorting out all the entry forms, and will probably have family and work commitments to contend with apart from organizing the cat show.

Miscellaneous and club classes are listed, in group sections, after the open classes. Again, make sure that you are entering the right classes. For example, in the British Shorthair section there will be classes for self cats – cats of a solid coat colour; a tabby entered in such a class would be disqualified as this coat pattern belongs in the non-self classes. Check and double-check the entry form to ensure all the information is correct, and that you have entered the right classes; remember to enclose your cheque for the entry fees, too, as no entry is accepted without the appropriate amount enclosed.

Lastly, it is advisable to enclose an SAE or postcard so that the show manager can let you know that your entry has been accepted – it is not much fun to drive a couple of hundred miles with a

RIGHT

At the end of the show day, the Best in Show judging takes place and the winning cats are placed in special pens for all to admire; this cat was the best rescued non-pedigree.

◈ EQUIPMENT NEEDED AT THE SHOW ◈

Although many shows have trade stands selling all the equipment needed for showing a cat, it is inadvisable to rely on this facility. Buy all that you will need in advance. Do not forget yourself either; most, but not all, show halls have catering facilities, so a packed lunch is often a good idea, and a folding chair as not all halls will provide adequate seating.

◗ The first essential is a sturdy cat carrier as no exhibit is accepted into the show hall uncontained; in the USA it is in fact acceptable, although a rarity, for cats to be confined on a collar and lead.

◗ In the UK all exhibits are in pens that are unmarked apart from their pen number. Each cat is allowed a plain, non-cellular blanket or piece of 'vetbed', a litter tray, water bowl and feeding dish, all of which must be plain white. In the USA, pens may be decorated and the equipment can be of any colour.

◗ The cats are all required to wear a tally bearing their pen number; the tally is provided, but the thin white ribbon or shirring elastic to put it on your cat is not.

◗ The pen that your cat will be confined to for the day has been cleaned and disinfected but many owners prefer to bring their own favourite disinfectant to be absolutely sure that the pen is safe.

◗ Do not forget cat litter and cat food – and the all-important can-opener if your cat's culinary preference is for the canned variety. Water is always available, but is often from non-mains water sources, so many exhibitors prefer to bring a small bottle of still mineral water for their cats.

◗ Lastly, all cats admitted to the show must have a current inoculation against FIE and, in the UK, the certificate of inoculation may need to be presented to the duty vet – so don't forget to pack the inoculation card with the show kit. Duty vets are rarely in attendance at shows in the USA.

ABOVE

At GCCF shows cats are all anonymous other than their pen number and have to be exhibited on a plain white blanket, with white litter tray and water bowl; the food bowl, seen in this pen, must be removed before the open class judging commences, as it could be construed as a distinguishing factor.

OPPOSITE

For show perfection, the coat of the British should be short, crisp and thick; many owners will allow their cats some outside access in order to crisp up the coat.

RIGHT

In most countries, cats must enter the show hall in a cat carrier. This top-of-the-range leather version may be the smartest way to travel, but any sturdy carrier would be equally suitable.

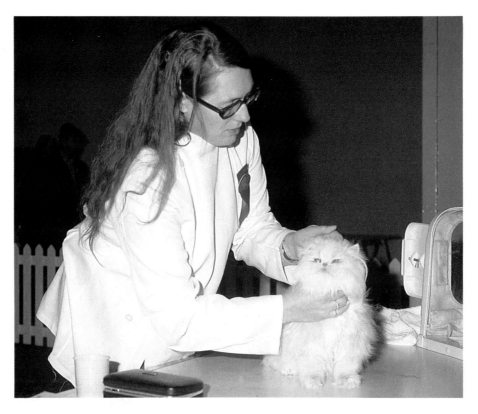

howling cat in the car only to discover that your cat is not entered as the entry form did not arrive, or arrived too late.

What to Do at a Show

Cat shows start early in the day, with the doors opening for the exhibitors and their cats around 7.30 am. The owner of each exhibit will be given a tally envelope, containing the pen number of the cat, a tally showing this number, and a prize money/rosette card. Some, usually the larger, shows send this to the exhibitor a week before the event, but at others this is the first thing to be collected on arrival at the show hall.

Next is vetting-in: all exhibits must be examined by one of the appointed veterinary surgeons before entering the main hall to be penned. The vet will examine the cat for any sign of parasites, such as fleas and ear mites, fungal infections like ringworm, and any infectious disease that could be transmitted at the show. Any cat found displaying symptoms of these has the alternative of being taken back home or being kept in the isolation room.

Safely through vetting-in, you will probably be given a 'V' card to display on your pen, signifying that your cat has passed the vet's examination. Some shows ask the vet to initial your tally envelope to indicate that the cat has been examined, and this is marked off on a chart with all the pen numbers. Whichever way, it ensures that only visibly fit and healthy exhibits enter the show hall.

RIGHT
A final brush and comb before the judging commences; with longhaired breeds, it is important that all traces of talcum powder are removed from the coat as this could lead to disqualification.

The next task is to find the pen with your cat's number on it. Clean the pen with disinfectant, if you have brought it, and leave the cat to settle in with its travelling blanket, litter tray, water and perhaps some food.

When the cat has settled in, you have a little time for some last-minute grooming; if your cat is longhaired, make sure that you have brushed out all traces of talcum powder from the coat. Then place the clean, white show blanket in the pen, and remove the travelling blanket and any container of food. Also remove any toys, or anything else that could be construed as a distinguishing feature. Do not forget to put the tally around the cat's neck or, if your cat is not used to a collar, the show manager may allow the tally to be tied on the pen; remember that a cat will not be judged unless the tally is attached to either cat or pen.

At 10.00 am all exhibitors are asked to leave the hall so that the judging of the all-important open classes can begin; they are then allowed back into the hall usually between noon and 12.30 pm.

As soon as the hall is cleared of exhibitors, the show catalogue will be available to all except the judges and their stewards. From this, you will be able to see exactly what competition your cat is facing and how many are in the various classes that you have entered.

The open class results will start coming up between 11.30 and noon, and as these are the most important classes there will be quite a crowd around the results board. The results slips are placed in numerical order of class, so are easy to locate. The slips themselves show only the pen number of the cat, again in numerical order, with the award number written at the side. This goes in order: 1, 2, 3, R (reserve or fourth), and the winners receive a rosette (some shows only award rosettes to the first three placings) and a prize card. In large classes of top-quality cats the judge may award further prizes of VHC (Very Highly Commended), HC (Highly Commended) and C (Commended) and the exhibit will be awarded a card to this effect.

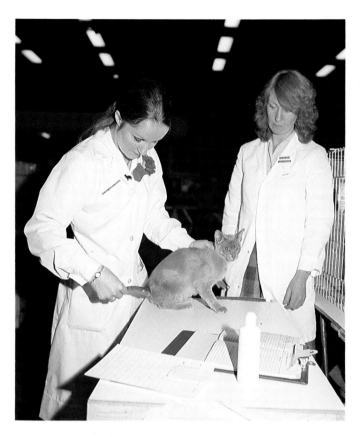

The winning male and female cats in the three opens (adult, kitten and neuter) for each particular breed and colour are then judged against each other for the Best of Breed rosette. Adults and neuters not entered in the open class, but only in the grand class, can also be considered for this award.

If the winning cat is up to the standards laid down, the result slip will indicate 'CC' (Challenge certificate) or 'PC' (Premier certificate) after the number 1; 'CC W/H' or 'PC W/H' shows that the judge has declined to award the certificate. It is possible that if the standard is too low the judge will withhold the first prize altogether, and '1 W/H' signifies this decision. 'CNH' against a pen number denotes the cat could not be handled. The rosettes and prize cards are then put on the pens in due course, but not until all the open class judging has been completed.

The side classes are judged after the opens; some shows will offer a choice

between prize money and rosettes, although most these days seem to just give rosettes. If there is a choice, you have to take your prize card to the rosette table in order to claim your preferred award.

At the end of the day some shows will hold a Best in Show competition ending up with the best adult, kitten and neuter in each of the seven sections and, if there is a non-pedigree section, a Best in Show Non-pedigree too. There are also cups available for club members to hold for one year; some shows will give them out on the day of the show, while others present these trophies at their annual general meetings.

SHOWS IN OTHER COUNTRIES

Throughout the world, the main objective of any cat show is to find the best example of each particular breed on the day of the show. These winning cats go on to win appropriate certificates that eventually afford them their respective championship status. The main differences between the UK and the rest of world lie in the way the shows are organized, the methods of judging, the recognized breeds eligible to enter championship classes, and the titles given to the winning cats. Also, British shows do not use the ring judging system and the pens are undecorated so that the cats have complete anonymity. Show preparation, schedules and entry forms, catalogues and the necessary equipment remain pretty much the same in whichever part of the world you show your cat.

American Shows

There are many governing bodies in the USA, all with different rules and regulations; some recognize certain breeds and colour patterns, and others do not. However, the main bodies are the Cat Fanciers Association (CFA) and The Independent Cat Association (TICA). Ring judging is the method used, so the cats'

◖ HOW THE JUDGES WORK ◗

In the UK the judge, accompanied by a steward, goes to the cat's pen; the steward is provided with a trolley so that the cat can be examined both in and out of the pen. The steward is also responsible for handling the cat and presenting it to the judge for his, or her, decision. In the USA and Europe, where ring judging is the main system, the steward's duties also include collecting each cat from its pen and delivering it to the judge in the appointed ring. The only time this happens in the UK is at the annual Supreme Cat Show, where a system of ring judging is also employed; the cats are brought to the judge, and the owners and members of the public are allowed to watch the judging. Because the judge never goes to the cats' pens these are allowed to be decorated, and any previous awards displayed for all to admire. To qualify to enter the Supreme, a cat has to already be a full Champion or Premier, or have gained at least one certificate in the previous show season; in the case of kittens, a win at a championship show secures entry. The highlight of the day is the final judging for the three Supreme winners: adult, kitten and neuter.

Pedigree cats are judged to the standards laid down for their particular breed and colour, but the condition, temperament, general health and presentation of the cat are also taken into consideration. If two cats are of similar quality, but one is groomed better, displays a sweeter disposition or even simply has a cleaner show blanket, this may well be reflected in the judge's placing of the exhibit. In the case of non-pedigree cats, where no 'standard of points' exists, these are the main criteria for the judging placements – along with a little subjective viewing on the part of the judge who may well prefer a tortie to a tabby!

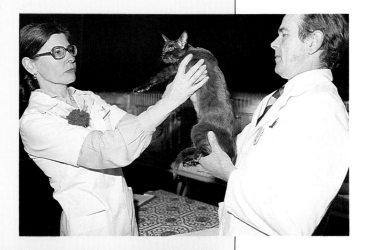

BELOW
The judge will need to assess the eye colour of each exhibit, and here the steward is holding the cat so the judge can look at the cat closely.

LEFT
Having assessed the finer points of the breed, the judge will wish to hold the cat in order to assess the weight, condition and general conformation of the cat.

● DIFFERENCES BETWEEN SHOWS IN UK, USA AND EUROPE ●

	UK (GCCF)	USA (general)	EUROPE (FIFe)
Exhibit to be registered in exhibitor's name	✓	✓	✓
Active/non-active register	✓	"NOT FOR BREEDING" MAY BE MARKED ON "BLUE SLIP"	✗
Vetting In	✓	✗	✓
Exhibits have to have been inoculated	✓	✓	FIFe REQUIRE INOCULATION AGAINST BOTH FIE & CAT FLU
Production of inoculation certificate	✓	✗	✗
Exhibits to be taken to show in carrier	✓	✗	✓
White show equipment needed	✓	✗	✗
Decorated pens allowed	ONLY AT SUPREME	✓	✓
Ring judging system	ONLY AT SUPREME	✓	✓
Pen judging system	✓	✗	✗
Open classes available	✓	✓	✓
Miscellaneous classes available	✓	✗	✗
CC, CAC, CACIB . . . certificates awarded	✓	✗	✓
Conferring of Champion/Premier title (3 shows/3 different judges)	✓	✗	✓
Can be made up to Champion at one show	✗	✓	✗
Judge's written report available on show day	ONLY AT SUPREME	✓	✓
Judge's written report published in specialist journal	✓	✗	✓
Cats/kittens may be purchased direct from show	✗	✓	✓

BELOW

In Europe, as in America, the pens are allowed to be decorated, as the judging takes place in a separate ring away from the area where the cats are penned.

pens can be highly decorated. The judging is an event that exhibitors and members of the public alike can sit and watch, with the judge giving a running commentary on the assessment of each exhibit. Unlike UK shows, a cat is entered in its breed class only. Under the CFA rules, a cat can become a Champion in a single show, and if the main judge thinks the cat of sufficient merit, two other judges will be asked to confirm the opinion and the award will be made.

Australian Shows

Shows in Australia are run very much in the same way as in Britain, with the judge going to the cat and not vice versa, and the pens are undecorated. The Australians are currently looking into the practicalities of ring judging but, for the present, abide by the GCCF system that the Co-ordinating Cat Council of Australia (CCCofA) has opted for.

European Shows

Clubs in Europe are mainly governed by the Fédération Internationale Féline (FIFe), the largest governing body on the Continent. Any shows run by FIFe-affiliated clubs have to abide by their rules in much the same way as the GCCF administers the rules of cat shows in Britain. Shows are all judged by the ring judging method, so the pens are usually highly decorated.

Cats are exhibited in the hope of winning a *Certificat d'Aptitude de Championnat* (CAC), the equivalent of the GCCF's Challenge certificate, or for those already made up to champions, a *Certificat d'Aptitude de Championnat International de Beauté* (CACIB), which is of the same status as the Grand Challenge certificate. Winning three certificates from three different judges, just as in the UK, entitles the cat to use the title Champion or, in the case of a CACIB, International Champion. There is no restriction on livestock being moved within European countries, and this title (the equivalent of Grand Champion in the UK) seems most suitable, as the most worthy of this honour have been shown in more than one country.

FIFe and the GCCF have considerable liaison, and it is quite common for British judges to adjudicate at Continental shows, and for FIFe judges to judge at the shows in the UK – the standard of points are all the same.

● THE JUDGES' REPORTS ●

The whole object of taking your cat to a show is to get an honest appraisal from the judges, so this is the single most important part of the whole day. All judges' reports in the UK are published in the weekly magazine Cats, *and the monthly magazine* Cat World *publishes a* Show World *section listing the winning cats, but without the judges' comments. It may be possible to talk to your judge during the show, but never interrupt a judge while he or she is still judging or your cat may be disqualified. (On receipt of an SAE, most judges are happy to send a copy of their report to you after the show.)*

The exception to this is the annual Supreme Show, and assessment classes in other shows, where the judges leave a written appraisal of each exhibit on the pen.

At FIFe shows, the judges provide a written report on the show day, and in America competitors have the best of both worlds – a running commentary while the judging is being carried out as well as a written score sheet itemizing how the points were awarded.

PREPARING YOUR CAT FOR THE SHOW

Show preparation is not something that can be achieved overnight by way of a miraculous transformation. A well cared-for cat should always look good, glowing with health, showing bright eyes and a glossy coat. This is dependent both on correct feeding and grooming, and the cat relies on its owner for these. Many an otherwise excellent breed specimen has been let down in this way, and nobody could possibly blame the cat. However, before the show there are a few little extra grooming procedures that can be followed – but remember that these will only enhance an otherwise well looked-after cat and will just add the finishing touches.

BELOW
Moisten the cat's coat with warm, not hot, water.

ABOVE
Rub the coat well with a non-allergenic shampoo.

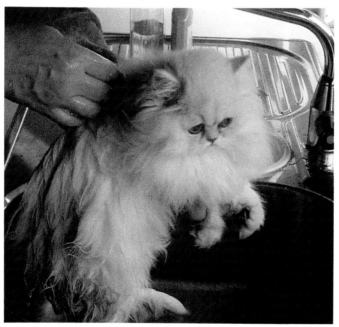

Washing Your Cat

All longhaired cats and some of the paler coloured shorthairs benefit from a bath a few days before the show. Unless your cat is accustomed to being bathed, it is advisable to have a friend with you to help. The kitchen sink is probably the best place to carry out this exercise; baths are too large and the cat can become frightened, and basins are too shallow.

● Fill the sink with warm water about one-third full. Using a shower rose attached to the tap, wet the cat's fur.

● Apply a small amount of non-stinging shampoo, such as a baby shampoo or one designed for cats. Gently rub through the coat, and rinse thoroughly. If there are any stubborn stains, repeat the process.

● Apply a good-quality hair conditioner, but try to avoid those with too much perfume in case this causes an allergic reaction. With longhaired cats, the addition of conditioner is vitally important, as it helps to separate the hairs, making the final grooming easier. Shorthairs need a little conditioner to prevent their sleek coats becoming too fluffy after washing.

● With a wide-toothed comb, work the conditioner through the coat, making sure that there are no matted parts remaining, and give a thorough rinse. Wrap the cat in a towel and rub well.

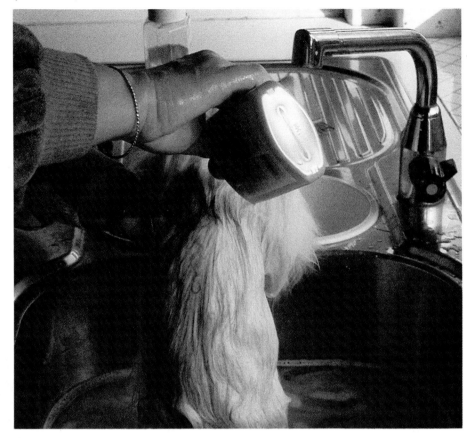

RIGHT
The addition of a good-quality hair conditioner will help free the coat of any tangles.

BELOW
Comb through the coat while the conditioner is still on.

BELOW
Finally, having rinsed the coat well, wrap the cat in a towel to take off the excess moisture.

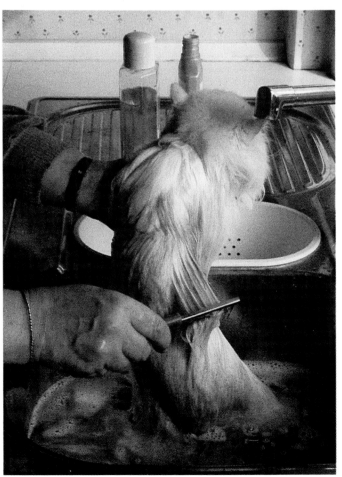

GIVING A BRAN BATH

For most shorthaired varieties, a bran bath can be beneficial. Warm some natural bran in the oven or microwave, until it is comfortably warm to the touch – never so hot that you burn your hands. Gently rub it right through the cat's coat. The bran will absorb any excess oils and loose dander. When brushed out well, this will leave the coat sparkling clean. A polish with a chamois leather or piece of silk will add a gleam to the fur.

1 Gently rub the warmed bran through the cat's coat.

2 Brush the bran out well for a sparkling clean coat.

Drying Your Cat

Next is the drying process and the way this is carried out differs between long-hair and shorthair varieties, as their fur texture is quite different. Whatever the type of cat, it is important to dry it as quickly as possible to prevent it catching a chill.

LONGHAIRED CATS. Many breeders of longhairs invest in a free-standing hair dryer, but these are expensive and an ordinary dryer can work just as well if you have a friend to hold it for you.

◖ Direct the hair dryer onto the cat's coat, but not so close as to cause discomfort. Using the wide-toothed comb, work your way through the coat, starting on the back and continuing through to the underparts.

◖ When the coat is semi-dry, sprinkle lightly with talcum powder, and start brushing with a bristle brush. Always work through the coat against the way it naturally lies, as this will add body and fullness.

◖ Continue like this until the cat is completely dry, adding extra powder as it is needed and making sure that the fur on the ruffs around the neck and the tail is well brushed up and free-flowing.

SHORTHAIRED CATS. Drying a shorthair cat is much simpler as the fur does not require powdering, and is meant to be close-lying.

◖ It is not necessary to use a hair dryer: if the cat objects, it can be towel-dried in front of a radiator or other heater.

◖ Always brush a shorthaired cat in the direction that the fur lies in order to keep the sleek appearance.

Final Checks

Lastly, make sure that the eyes and ears are clean. Any trace of 'sleep' around the eye can be removed with a clean finger. A cotton bud wiped inside the outer part of the ear will ensure that these are quite

clean too. Indeed, all orifices should be completely clean – there are certain things that judges prefer not to find on their hands! Finally, clip the cat's claws just enough to blunt the tips – no judge likes being scratched, and even a friendly pet can accidentally draw blood if the claws are left long.

ABOVE
After bathing a cat, especially if it is a longhaired variety, it is important to dry the coat as quickly as possible so that the cat does not get chilled.

◖ AFTER THE SHOW ◖

Whatever precautions have been taken to minimize the chance of infection being passed from one cat to another, there is always a slight risk of your cat bringing back something it didn't leave home with – and not just a certificate. In a multi-cat household, especially if there are young, un-inoculated kittens in the home, do take care. Some exhibitors will go as far as isolating any cat returning from a show, which may seem a sensible precaution. Certainly, a quick dose of flea spray before the cat is allowed in with other cats will ensure that none of those

unwelcome visitors get any further.

An old-fashioned idea that does work is to soak a piece of cotton wool in whisky, or some other alcohol, and swab inside the cat's mouth, paws and anal region; alcohol kills most germs, and these parts of the anatomy are most likely to be exposed to infection.

It is also a sensible precaution for exhibitors who have young un-inoculated kittens at home, to disinfect their hands and shoes before touching any cats in their household. Even better, change your clothing and shoes. This is not extreme advice, just common sense.

FURTHER READING

Andrews, Tony Dr, and Humphreys, David Dr. *Poisoning in Veterinary Practice.* Noah, 3 Crossfield Chambers, Gladbeck Way, Enfield, UK.

Black's Veterinary Dictionary. A C Black, London.

Brown, Carol V. *The Pieces of a Cat.* Carlton Press, Inc, New York.

Cutts, Paddy. *The Essential Cat.* Brian Trodd, London.

Fogarty, Marna (Ed). *The Cat Fanciers' Association, Inc 1991–1992 Yearbook.* CFA, Inc, Manasquan, NJ, USA.

Fogel, Bruce. *Know Your Cat: An Owner's Guide to Cat Behavior.* Dorling Kindersley, New York and London.

Fogel, Bruce. *The Cat's Mind.* Pelham Books, London.

Hawcroft, Tim. *Complete Book of Cat Care.* Ring Press Books, Letchworth, Herts, UK.

Hornidge, Marilis. *That Yankee Cat, The Maine Coon.* Tilbury House Publishers, Gardiner, ME, USA.

Kunkel, Paul. *How to Toilet Train Your Cat: 21 Days to a Litter-free Home.* Workman Publishing, New York.

MacDonald, Mardie. *The Cat Psychologist.* Perigee Books, New York.

Moore, Joan. *Cat Shows and Showing Cats.* Cat World Ltd, Shoreham-by-Sea, W Sussex, UK.

Pedersen, Neils C. *Feline Husbandry, Diseases and Management in the Multiple Cat Environment.* American Veterinary Publications, Goleta, CA, USA.

Pocock, Robine. *The Burmese Cat.* BCC c/o Mrs Boizard-Neil, Willow House, Rowe Lane, Pirbright, Surrey, UK.

Prosé, Pieter J. *Practical Cat Genetics for the Breeders of Persian Cats.* Dutch and English versions c/o Mme Helene Prosé, Gastelseweg 45, 6021 GK Budel, Netherlands.

Robinson, Roy. *Genetics for Cat Breeders.* Pergamon Press, Oxford, UK.

Simmonet, Jean. *The Chartreux Cat.* Synchro Company of Paris; c/o Jerome M Auerback, 823 Debra St, Livermore, CA, USA.

Simpson, Michael and Patricia (Eds). *Caring For, Breeding, and Showing Your Maine Coon Cat.* Maine Coon Breeders & Fanciers Assoc, c/o Patricia Simpson, 13283 Deron Avenue, San Diego, CA 92129, USA.

Smith, Vivienne. *The Birman Cat.* c/o Bridge House, 2 Gold Street, Riseley, Bedfordshire, UK.

Stephens, Gloria. *Legacy of the Cat.* Chronicle Books, San Francisco, CA, USA.

Tabor, Roger. *The Rise of the Cat.* BBC Publications, London.

Tellington-Jones, Linda, with Taylor, Sybil. *The Tellington TTouch: A Breakthrough Technique to Train and Care for Your Favorite Animal.* Jane Wesman Public Relations for the Arts, New York.

Turner, Dennis C. *The Domestic Cat: Biology of its Behaviour.* Cambridge University Press, Cambridge, UK.

Vella, Carolyn M, and McGonagle, John J. *In the Spotlight.* Howell Book House, Macmillan Publishers Co., New York.

Wright, Michael, and Walters, Sally (Eds). *The Book of the Cat.* Pan Books, London and Sydney.

USEFUL ADDRESSES

A list of the official organisations of the major international cat fancies, together with their official or semi-official journals.

AUSTRALIA

Co-ordinating Cat Council of Australia (CCCofA)
Box No 4317 GPO
Sydney
NSW 2001

Council of Federated Cat Clubs of Queensland
c/o Secretary
June E Lobwein
19 Clifford St
Toowoomba 4350

Feline Association of South Australia
c/o Secretary
Mr Lee Caldwell
21 Poole St
Osborne 5015

Feline Control Council of Queensland
c/o Secretary
Mrs A Barrett
84 Anzac Ave
Redcliffe 4020

Feline Control Council of Victoria (RAS)
c/o Secretary
Mrs Marion Jones
Royal Showground
Epsom Road
Ascot Vale 3032

Governing Council of the Cat Fancy in Victoria
c/o Secretary
Mrs Sandra Weaver-Hall
PO Box 73
Oakleigh 3166

Murray Valley Cat Authority
c/o Secretary
Miss Shirley E Osmond
PO Box 406
Mildura 3500

Queensland Independent Cat Council
c/o Secretary
Miss Pat Mercer
PO Box 41
Esk 4312

RNCAS Cat Club
c/o Mr Bjorn Christie-Johnston
PO Box 404
Dickson 2602

JOURNAL

Royal Agricultural Society Cat Control Journal
Box No 4317 GPO
Sydney
NSW 2001

EUROPE

Fédération Internationale Féline (FIFe)
c/o Secretary
Mme R van Haeringen
23 Doerhavelaan
Eindhoven 5644 BB
Netherlands

JOURNAL

A Tout Chat
(*service des abonnements –*
subscriptions)
BP 205
Versailles 78003
France

SOUTH AFRICA

Governing Council of the Associated Cat Clubs of South Africa
c/o Mrs M Simpson
45 Edison Drive
Meadowridge 7800

All Breeds Cat Club
PO Box 1078
Cape Town 8000

Cat Fanciers' Club of South Africa
PO Box 783100
Sandton 2146

Eastern Province Cat Club
PO Box 5166
Walmer 6065

Natal Cat Club
100 Marian Hill Road
Ashley
Pinetown 3610

Rand Cat Club
PO Box 180
Springs 1560

Transvaal Cat Society
PO Box 13385
Northmead 1511

Western Province Cat Club
PO Box 3600
Cape Town 8000

UNITED KINGDOM

Governing Council of the Cat Fancy (GCCF)
4–6 Penel Orlieu
Bridgewater
Somerset TA6 3PG

GCCF Cat Welfare Liaison Committee
c/o Secretary
Mrs Barbara Harrington
79 Pilgrim's Way
Kemsing
Near Sevenoaks
Kent TB15 6TD

Feline Advisory Bureau
350 Upper Richmond Road
Putney
London SW15 6TL

JOURNALS

Cats
5 James Leigh St
Manchester M1 6EX

Cat World
10 Western Road
Shoreham-by-Sea
West Sussex BN4 5WD

UNITED STATES

American Cat Association (ACA)
8101 Katherine Drive
Panorama City
CA 91402

American Cat Fanciers' Association (ACFA)
PO Box 203
Point Lookout
MO 65726

Cat Fanciers' Association (CFA Inc)
PO Box 1005
Manasquan
NJ 087361005

Cat Fanciers' Federation (CFF)
9509 Montgomery Road
Cinncinatti
OH 45242

The Independent Cat Association (TICA)
PO Box 2988
Harlingen
TX 87550

JOURNALS

Cat Fancy
PO Box 4030
San Clemente
CA 92672

Cats
445 Merrimac Drive
Port Orange
FL 32019

Cat World
PO Box 35635
Phoenix
AZ 850969

INDEX

ACKNOWLEDGEMENTS

My most grateful thanks to my editor LESLEY ELLIS who has helped to make this book much more readable and to JUDITH SIMONS and JOANNA LORENZ of ANNESS PUBLISHING LTD for their help and support.

ROY ROBINSON F.I.BIOL. who advised me on genetics and checked related text.

My veterinary surgeon, JOHN OLIVER B.VET.MED., MRCVS, for his advice and help in ensuring the veterinary facts are as up to date and accurate as possible.

LESLEY PRING and the staff of the GCCF for their advice on cat breeds.

LARRY JOHNSON, for supplying photographs of American breeds that do not yet exist in the UK.

DAPHNE NEGUS for her advice on the Pan-American aspects of the Cat Fancy.

MARJORIE HORNETT for allowing me to photograph her Bengal and Ocicat, and for the valuable information she provided on these breeds.

SUE KEMPSTER (British), SALLY FRANKLIN (Orientals), DAVID FROUD (Maine Coons), ANGELA SIVYER (Manx) and ALAN WATTS (Norwegian Forest Cats) for their help in providing suitable cats of their respective breeds for photography.

SAL MARSH for her help on the Breeding chapter.

ROSEMARY ALGER for reading through the manuscript to check for any omissions.

BARBRO MAGNUSSON and HAZEL GLOVER for lending me their respective cats for the step-by-step grooming sequences.

LYNDA TAYLOR and the LYNCHARD CHINCHILLAS.

SUSIE MORSE for her help with the word processing.

AQUAPETS (EALING) LONDON for the loan of equipment needed for photography.

COLOUR CENTRE (LONDON) LTD for processing transparencies with their usual care and efficiency.

TERRY MOORE of the CAT SURVIVAL TRUST, Welwyn, Herts.

MIRANDA VON KIRCHBERG for valuable information on the Burmilla/Asian breeding programme.

Lastly, my grateful thanks to my friend LYNN VAN HAEFTEN who has kindly done my shopping, errand running and kept me supplied with everything I needed while writing this book!

• CREDITS •

Photographs by Paddy Cutts, Animals Unlimited. The publishers and author would like to thank the following for additional picture material: Cat Survival Trust, page 12; E T Archives, pages 8–9; Larry Johnson, pages 131 *t*, 161 *b*, 170 *tl*, 171 *c*, 177, 192, 193, 197, 198, 205 *t*, 213 *b*, 223; Sal Marsh, page 97; Dr K L Thoday, Royal (Dick) School of Veterinary Studies, University of Edinburgh, pages 118 *bl*, 120 *tr*; Murray Thomas, back jacket flap; Edward Young, pages 30, 238, 240 *t*.